The Rebirth, the inner true life, or how do humans become blessed?

In accordance with the words of sacred scripture and the laws of thinking

answered by a freemason
(attributed to Karl Kolb)

The Rebirth, the inner true life, or how do humans become blessed?

In accordance with the words of the sacred scripture and the laws of thinking

answered by a freemason
(attributed to Karl Kolb)

translated by Kerry A Nitz

K A Nitz
AUCKLAND, NEW ZEALAND

*Die Wiedergeburt, das innere wahrhaftige Leben,
oder wie wird der Mensch selig?*
published in German 1857 and
attributed to Karl Kolb

This translation into New Zealand English
Copyright © K A Nitz 2023
All rights reserved

ISBN: 978-0-473-67867-8

Table of Contents

Translator's Note..7
Motto..9
Foreword..11
Part 1: The Theory of Life..13
Part 2: The Methods for the Inner Life...27
Part 3: The Evidence of Sacred Scripture.......................................57
About the Author...105

Translator's Note

For the English translation of Bible texts I have made use of the King James Version. Where I thought it would be helpful I have also inserted missing Biblical citations in the footnotes.

Motto

If you want, friend, to fly to the sublimest heights of wisdom,
Dare it at the risk that prudence laughs at you.
The short-sighted see only the shore that draws you back,
Not where your brave flight will one day land.
Schiller

Foreword

1. Orthodoxy and rationalism stand opposed to one another without either the one or the other party endeavouring to find a common basis for their views.
2. As long as this does not happen, a final adjudication is impossible — for until then both sides fight each other with weapons which are incapable of injuring the weaknesses of the other.
3. Orthodoxy fights with Bible texts to which the rationalist grants no validity.
4. The rationalist fights by contrast with grounds based on reason which orthodoxy considers incompetent next to the Bible.
5. Both sides are wrong to the degree they fail to recognise the responsibility of establishing a foundation which contradicts neither the Bible nor healthy human reason, and thereby enables the brusque conflicts of both factions to be delivered before a common seat of judgement.
6. If orthodoxy will not endeavour to find such a common basis, then it will degenerate into fanaticism and, instead of awakening a lively faith, will finally ossify into dead observance.
7. If rationalism fails to recognise this responsibility, then it will degenerate into the desire for money and honour, that is, into sophisticated sensuality, and sink into indifference with respect to God and eternity.
8. Service to forms and half-heartedness are two equally pitiful consequences. Both carry the religious need of humanity to the grave and expose the latter to the danger of an ossification like that we perceive in almost all Asiatic peoples.
9. The author acknowledges Bible and reason as legitimate and has endeavoured to deliver in the following treatise the proof that both authorities can be brought together with the same means to the same goal.
10. The following treatise shall thus be an attempt at establishing a common forum for the brusque conflicts of strict be-

liefs and reason. The treatise itself breaks down into three parts.

11. In the first part, under the heading of **The Theory of Life**, I have systematically discussed the goal of human existence on the grounds of reason.

12. In the second part, under the heading **The Methods for the Inner Life**, I have specified the ways and means for how humans can achieve the final aim of their lives.

13. In the first and second parts, I have indeed cited many Bible texts — however not in order to prove things with them, but rather merely to cite Bible texts running parallel with my assertions.

14. In the third part finally, under the heading **The Evidence of Sacred Scripture**, I have shown the congruence of my propositions with the words of sacred scripture.

15. If I have succeeded in this, then I have delivered thereby the proof that between *rationalism* and *orthodoxy* — between *pantheism* and *deism* — a different view is yet possible which may be able to reconcile both extreme factions.

16. According to the words of Christ there is to be *one* shepherd and *one* flock.

17. As long as Christianity follows the paths trod up to now, this prophecy will not be fulfilled.

18. The present process not only leaves no hope that the Jews, Muslims, Indians, and Chinese shall ever become converted to Christ — no, it will not even prevent that even within Christianity new splits, quarrels, sects, and schisms will constantly emerge.

19. The error of this wrong beginning, however, does not lie in the people — but rather in the teachers and leaders themselves. Hence, this text is directed primarily at the latter, and if it contributes even only a mite to Christian unity, then the publication of this text will appear justified.

20. Clear cognition is necessary in all things — but most of all in the most important affair of human life. To strive for this was the intention of the author.

Part 1: The Theory of Life

21. The theory of life is based on the following two principles which are recognised by healthy human reason as a thing that goes without saying:

22. I. There is a cause for all things and we call this original cause "God".

23. II. God is absolutely perfect; he is qualitatively indivisible and quantitatively immeasurable.

24. Everything that fulfills his goal is perfect. God as cause of all things can aim at nothing more than himself. He achieves this aim in every direction, consequently he is absolutely perfect.

25. In terms of quality, he is indivisible because no divisible quality can be the cause of *all* things.

26. In terms of quantity, he is immeasurable because if a cause had been present which bounded him, then God would not be the cause of all things.

27. We will return later to the nature of God and seek to define this nature, in so far as it is nothing but vain power; but first the relationship in which the human spirit stands with God must be discussed.

28. All things are differentiated in material and form.

29. With respect to the material, we must consider the human spirit as a ray of the divine spirit because it is supernatural like God.

30. With respect to the form, identity with God likewise reigns because we see in the human spirit the highest characteristics of God: wisdom, beauty, and strength.

31. On this basis, a third principle is revealed:

III. The human spirit is a part of God.

32. If the human spirit were not a part of God, then it would have to be something different. And what? A part of some other being? What existence, what being outside of God, however, possesses will, consciousness, and power of thought?!

33. In the creation story of Genesis, it says:

"And the Lord God formed man of the dust of the ground, and breathed into his nostrils the breath of life; and man became a living soul." — Genesis 2:7

Can this breath of life be something other than a part of God? Does this breath not have to be a part of God in order to make humans in the image of God?!

34. Some claim that God created the human spirit out of nothing. This claim is almost too vapid and only deserves a mention because the misunderstanding of the following text could give cause for that:

"Through faith we understand that the worlds were framed by the word of God, so that things which are seen were not made of things which do appear." — Hebrews 11:3[*]

Under the "not made of things" in the preceding text, however, it is not abstract things that is to be understood, but rather "not made of earthly, material things", for it is said expressly at the start: the worlds were framed *by the word of God.*

35. If it is definite, however, that the human spirit is a part of God, then it goes without saying that the human ego cannot be identical with the spirit. For if the spirit is a part of God, then it is existing for eternity, but the human has a beginning, consequently there is a difference between human and spirit, and we need to ask of what the human ego, one's individuality consists?

36. A fourth principle is now revealed:

IV. The human ego is the product of the connection of spirit and body.

37. The human ego is neither identical with the spirit, nor with the body. — Not with the spirit because that is for eternity, and not with the body because that is surely still present in death, but the ego has vanished.

38. No other way out therefore remains than to seek the ego in the connection of spirit and body, and it will be good to make this relationship visible by a few parallels, which is not difficult since here all nature delivers analogies.

---

[*] [Tr.: in the German Bible of Luther the last phrase translates literally as "everything you see came from nothing".]

39. All chemical combinations are indeed (because in too lower a sphere) weak parallels, but make visible though how from a connection entirely new bodies can emerge with entirely new characteristics and powers. Water, for example, is the combination of two gases of which each one has no similarity with water.

40. A more rewarding parallel is a musical instrument, e.g. a recorder. This may be considered a combination of wood and music. The recorder is not wood and not music, but rather a tool by which the spirit of music is revealed. Similarly humans are not body and not spirit, but rather the human body is a tool by which the spirit of God is revealed.

41. This parallel can be extended as far as the moral (ethical) sphere. Let's suppose the case that the recorder is somehow neglected so that it gives discordant tones. These discordant tones, however, are not the consequence of the music, nor the wood — but rather the consequence of change in those relationships under which the wood is a recorder. Likewise if humans somehow become imperfect, infirm, faulty — then the spirit, the part of God, is also not thereby altered, but rather only those relationships under which a body is a human.

42. Every mistake, every sin alters humans in their connection as a human — but not in their life-spirit which as a part of God is, on account of its eternal nature, not subject to any change or transformation.

43. The human spirit is as a part of God absolutely perfect to the extent God is qualitatively indivisible. The human spirit therefore knows all things of itself, because everything as an idea was contained in it eternally. The human spirit therefore does not need eyes to see, nor ears to hear, it lives in eternal clairvoyance. It therefore needs no doctrine and no teaching. It cannot become wiser, nor more foolish. It is what it is, what it was, and what it will be. It cannot invent anything new and cannot forget anything old, for it is the old and new itself. For it there is no progress and no regress — for its nature is eternally stable to the extent the perfect is beyond ferment and metamorphosis.

44. Therefore the expressions like "enlightened spirit", "mentally ill", "absent minded"* are also just as inessential as "sunrise, sunset, solar eclipse" and the like.

45. Humans bear the highest being within themselves — but they are this highest being as little as the recorder is music, and all afflictions do not become a burden on the spirit of God, but rather on the human.

46. One takes a masterwork, e.g. a clock; it goes infallibly, like the sun. But through use the mechanism by and by wears out, and after a number of years it is seen to go wrong. This is the image of humans who become in their old age weak and dulled. The fallible action of the clock is not the consequence of the mechanics. The clock goes wrong not because the laws of mechanics have been adulterated, but rather because its tools have become unusable. Likewise with a weak-minded old man the spirit has not suffered hardship, but rather the organs by which the spirit reveals itself.

47. A crystal clear water can be made murky by filth. Thus the human spirit which in respect to its nature is pure and honest, like the sunlight, often appears impure and unclean as soon as the human introduces the filth of earthly greed into his disposition. All that does not besmirch the spirit though, but rather only the human in his connection as human.

48. Since the human spirit is a part of God, it also cannot sleep, cannot faint, cannot lose consciousness as little as the stone can ever stop being heavy. Sleep, unconsciousness, stupidity, etc., etc. are not spiritual — but rather human states, states which find their explanation in the modification of that connection in which the spirit and body are a human.

49. Were that not the case, then human and spirit would have to be identical. Were the ego identical with the spirit, however, then the ego would have to know what spirit is, because an innate thing cannot be in ignorance of itself. But then the spirit is indeed a puzzle for us, it is indeed unbeknown to us. The unbeknown must, however, be another thing than that which just wants to get to know this unbeknown.

---

* [Tr.: the German word for spirit, *Geist*, is also used for intellect or mind. So, for instance, *Geisteskrank* = illness of spirit/mind = mentally ill. Hence, wherever spirit is used here, it may contain this double-meaning.]

50. Assuming (but never admitting) that the human is identical with his spirit and this spirit is created by God out of nothing — then indeed the human spirit would be a self-contained whole. It would have been pure nonsense to capture this independent being in a frail body; the extent to which the human could find himself ignorant over his spiritual capabilities could not be overlooked; furthermore it would be incomprehensible as to why the human only develops gradually, since he would be identical with the spirit and this spirit emerges fully formed from the hand of God. Indeed still more — if the human is identical with his spirit and this spirit is created specially by God, then indeed the divinity bears the responsibility that he gifted one human, restricted another, that one is demure, the other impudent. The rejection of principles III and IV would lead to such inconsistencies.

51. But if both these principles are well-founded in the nature of the matter and hence humans are nothing more than connections, then the individuality must expire in death — provided that with corporeal life a *new connection* was not produced which, as soon as the earthly body breaks up, can take the ego into itself.

52. Humans find themselves therefore (if at any rate in a different sphere) precisely in a similar state to that in which the egg or the caterpillar finds itself.

53. Should the talk thus be of immortality, then we must investigate whether the possibility of a new connection is present, so that when the human dies as caterpillar, he can continue a new existence as a butterfly.

54. To this end we must subject the dream life to an examination. The dream could not at all take place in and of itself if human and spirit were identical. For if the will of the spirit and of the human were identical, how could some activity of fantasy make itself known against our will! Thus here a similar phenomenon appears as with the motions of many bodily muscles, like the heart, stomach, lungs, etc., which also move without any action of the human will and which thus prove just like the the dream life the conclusiveness of principle IV.

55. In dream itself there are two things to distinguish:
    1. the images or apparitions,
    2. the senses which perceives these images.

The images are of a confused, chaotic nature, and since these images, as is claimed, lack reality, it is generally believed that the dream and what connects with it are not worthy of the consideration of a rational man. Although the images may be really or imaginarily present, in no way does a difficulty arise for the *sense* which perceives these images. In order to perceive the image in a mirror, the eye is just as much necessary as with the original. The ability to gaze must be completely developed, no matter whether I want to perceive something real or something imaginary. Moreover you will surely have to concede that every appearance assumes a reality which causes this appearance. E.g. in a room closed off by shutters, into which the light can only penetrate through a few cracks, you will see on the covers all the persons who walk past on the street, likewise moving, but transformed perversely. Now admittedly these baroque images on the covers are only appearance — although the appearance itself is real — and can only be produced by the person really walking past on the street. The baroque dream images are quite similar phenomena; they too could not have arisen without a real something, and since this something does not find its basis in the will of the individual, another self-acting power must yet be present, and this power I call the "inner life".

56. Since now the human can see, hear, feel, smell, and taste in the dream, whilst the external senses though are closed, the dream forms the proof that in the inner nature of the human another life is present which entitles us to put forward the fifth principle:

57. V. The possibility of a new connection — (inner life) — is vouched for by dreams.

58. The vague consciousness, the limited intelligence, can by rights be simply explained by that the usual human in the dream sphere or in the inner life finds themselves on a similar level as the newborn child in outer life.

59. Analogous with the dream is the following experiment: someone goes at midday into a dark chamber and endeavours there in upright position to think of nothing. You will soon soon see the insolubility of this task; for you will find that the stiller and calmer the outer human becomes, the more lively it becomes in the inner. Were spirit and human one, then it

would have to be possible for the latter to think of *nothing*; since that is not the case, this experiment, which anyone can carry out, is also a proof that behind the surface of everyday life yet another is hidden, and this other life I call the *inner life*.

60. Now since the earthly body, like all earthly material, is subjected to constant change and transformation, since the human organs gradually wear out into unusability, since moreover the individuality must expire with death, even because the human ego exists only in the *connection* of spirit and body, the human must, if he wants otherwise to realise the wish for *eternal* happiness, produce in bodily life a new sounder connection in himself, and since according to principle V the *possibility* is present here, a further principle is thus revealed:

61. VI. To have the inner life produce and develop itself is the purpose of humans.

62. Many think this new connection, this new spiritual body, the inner life forms itself by itself. — No analogy in all of nature justifies such a hypothesis. — The power of the spirit of the workmaster who builds the new body like the earthly one in the womb is good — but provided that the human eludes the influence of this spirit, provided that he does not devote himself to the activity of this spirit and does not bring to the new human, to the inner life, the suitable nourishment — then it can be impossible for a new connection to come into being.

63. The human must produce the inner life in himself, and as soon as this new human is fit for life, he must be born once more. Without rebirth there can be no talk of a life on the other side, of a life on the other side of the grave, of immortality.

64. The rebirth, however, is a two-fold one:
   1. a corporeal one,
   2. a moral one.

65. As in the earthly life, in the marriage at first the physical existence and only afterwards the moral education of the children is striven for, so too is it in the spiritual. In the place of the frail earthly body a new unbreakable body formed from spiritual materials must appear. Likewise though all sinful

and earthly desires and life's urges must also die because they would not find any nourishment anymore on the other side.

66. From the nature of the thing it follows by itself, however, that the bodily rebirth must precede the moral; indeed still more, that the bodily rebirth will perhaps always draw the moral after itself. For the caterpillar, even if it also lives so respectably, is and remains a caterpillar. The butterfly by contrast, as soon as it just once feels the power of its new wings tinged with the colours of the ether, and tastes nectar and ambrosia from the flowers and blossoms, it will not think at all anymore of crawling on the ground and eating dust. How can a human, as soon as free spiritual powers awaken in him, still cling with lust and yearning to the transient? Like a grown-up smiles at the toys of children and no longer comprehends how he once long ago could also take pleasure in them, so does the reborn smile at the wealth, the might, the honour and vanity of the world, and does not comprehend anymore how these playthings of humans could divert from his true purpose, from the flight to heaven, his eternal home.

67. If it is now according to principle VI the purpose of the human to develop in themselves the inner life (the butterfly), then a precise definition of the inner life must be given to the human so that he possesses in this definition an ideal which he can take as a model, possess a touchstone by which he can ascertain the state of his inner life.

68. Now although this ideal originally lived in the breast of humans, like the instinct in animals, the sensual earthly nature gradually won the upper hand in such a way that even the faith in the life on the other side suffered a shipwreck. Despite all religious laws, doctrines, and commandments, humans sank ever deeper down into sensuality. The world shackled them with thousands of bonds, and the idea, the concept of the inner life would have finally turned completely into an hypothesis, into a fairy tale, so that finally all humans would have died in their sins (i.e. lacking the inner life), if a saviour in the person of Christ, a rescuer had not come who possessed the inner life in such maturity, perfection, and completeness that he could not just pronounce a cold bare theory (whose real practical worth you could have doubted,

disputed), but rather could pronounce *himself* as living example, as representation — as definition of the true inner life.

69. Accordingly the seventh principle is finally revealed:

VII. The true inner life in its highest perfection and maturity is represented by the life of Jesus.

70. But now if Christ is the representative of the true inner life, the four gospels draw up a glorious image of the nature, of the powers, and of the effectiveness of the inner life.

71. The spiritual senses of Christ were so developed that he could see and hear with their help events of the past, present, and future. With his spiritual ear he heard the utterances of all the prophets who prophesied him. With his inner eye he foresaw the destruction of Jerusalem, and his suffering and dying. With his inner senses he saw Nathaniel under the fig tree, saw the donkey which was handed over to his disciples on the words: the Lord needs it*. With his spiritual senses he read the hearts of the sick, saw their broken disposition, and said, be of good cheer; thy sins be forgiven thee†.

72. He not only possessed physically himself the fullness of health, but also shared it with others. His word, his laying on of hands, indeed even the touch of his clothes had healing power. Thus the blind started seeing, the deaf hearing, the lame walking, the leprous became clean, the gouty well, and every cripple healthy — indeed even the dead returned to life.

73. To the poor the gospel of salvation, the prospect of a happy existence was announced, for he preached powerfully.

74. The here and now and the other side had no partition wall for him, he spoke with Moses and Elijah over the end he should take.

75. The elements submitted to him; he commanded the storms with power and a great stillness occurred.

76. His spirit prevailed already in the here and now over the weight of his earthly body so that he could walk on water without danger.

77. He stopped the eyes of his adversaries so they did not see him. For when they wanted to stone him, he walked through the middle of the crowd brushing past them.

---

*   [Tr.: Matthew 21:3.]
†   [Tr.: Matthew 9:2.]

78. He was capable of physically satisfying not only himself through the *word*, but thousands of people.

79. His inner life heard the quietest vibrations of the spirit; he could speak in all situations and relationships with God, his father, and desire of him advice, consolation, and help.

80. And he promised all these glorious powers and divine capabilities for the inner life, for which the following texts amongst many others provide evidence.

81. "If ye abide in me, and my words abide in you, ye shall ask what ye will, and it shall be done unto you." — John 15:7, the like in Matthew 17:20. — Matthew 21:22. — Matthew 18:19. Mark 11:24. Mark 16:17 — 18. — Matthew 7:8. Mathew 7:11. Luke 17:6. John 14:14, etc.

82. That is the enormous difference between external and inner life, that the faith of outer life is powerless and feeble, a mere opinion, like chaff in the wind. — The faith of the inner life by contrast is a magical power, is divine strength which knows no obstacle and does not rest until fulfillment nears. Almighty God speaks to the faith of the inner life: are you perhaps too afraid to believe in me! Behold the height of the stars* and show me the bounds of my omnipotence!!! — — —

83. Humans are born pietists, i.e. humans always believe they must win God's favour by their gestures, by their constant praying, begging, and pleading. — The essence of pietism consists thus, even if in an unacknowledged way, in its logical consequence in that God is imagined as an indeed omnipotent, but hard-hearted being who is only moved by constant, if need be wretched whimpering to pity and help. — This idea is a perverse one. Humans can surely by days, weeks, months, and years of prayer, vigil, and fasting beg for much from the Creator (Matthew 17:21), but the exaltation does not follow because God is finally weakened by the wailing, but rather because the inner life has been forcefully spiralled upwards by the constant vigil, prayer, and fasting. — Provided, however, that the human, in times when it goes well for him, where no worry, no sorrow, no misery burdens his heart, seeks and awakes the inner life, then in the case of hardship he does not need such horrible efforts; he sends his request through his

---

* [Tr.: cf. Job 22:12.]

inner life, through Christ in him to the Father, and the hearing is as certain: as those who have learnt something in their youth are certain that they will not go hungry in old age — as certain as you concentrate the rays of the sun by means of a magnifying glass and can thereby ignite a spark — as certain as with the touch of positive and negative electricity lightning and thunder follows, etc. — Here all brooding and disputation is superfluous. Experience is the mother of science. You are convinced by an experiment, and you will reach your goal more certainly than through any meditation. Hence away with all pietism. Get to work, awake the inner life, then you humans will be behaving worthy of your divine descent.

84. It is moreover written that in the inner life everyone will be taught by God. For anyone who hears the word of the Father and learns it will arrive at the inner life. John 6:45. Luke 12:12. John 16:13. John 14:26. 2 Peter 1:21. Matthew 10:20. Mark 13:11. Luke 21:15.

85. The inner life perceives the finest vibrations of the spirit, thus stands in immediate rapport with God and can thus draw ever new instruction from God himself; can speak with God and turn in all the affairs of life to Him, his Father, his best friend in order to ask for advice, consolation, and help.

86. "He that believeth on me, the works that I do shall he do also; and greater works than these shall he do; because I go unto my Father." John 14:12. Matthew 24:47. Matthew 9:8. Luke 10:19.

87. The crown of all glorious deeds remains however Christ's resurrection and ascension. He thereby just delivered the perfect proof of the possibility of an eternal happy existence.

88. Therefore the wisdom of God says *go and do the same* and John closes his gospel with the words:

89. And there are also many other things which Jesus did, the which, if they should be written every one, I suppose that even the world itself could not contain the books that should be written. Amen.[*]

90. These concerns were only too convincing. You don't even comprehend the books anymore. To one person the works of Christ are symbols and devout parables. To another they are

---
[*] [Tr.: John 21:25.]

expressions of divine omnipotence. Both views are erroneous. Humans cannot do the works of Christ, but surely the spirit of God which the human bears within himself and with which he shall identify through the rebirth can.

91. What sort of a Christianity is it if we praise Christ with full cheeks (Matthew 7:21) and are not capable of doing the tiniest of his works!!! Matthew 7:15–16. Should then Christ be and remain amongst all the so-called Christians the only true Christian?!! Matthew 12:50.

92. Fulfill public duties, go to church and to communion, give alms, join a society for missionary work or for other charitable purpose, make devout gestures, found benevolent endowments for widows and orphans or the like, those are things the scoundrel can do just as well as the honourable man. (Cf. Matthew 9:5.) But make the sick healthy through the word of God, stop infectious disease through the power of the word, prevent meagre growth, flooding, see into the future, speak with God, recognise the thoughts of another, walk on water, drink something deadly without detriment, travel to heaven and the like, only the true Christian who is born again in Christ can, only the Christ in us, the inner life, can. —

93. That is that good work of which Christ speaks: Let your light so shine before men, that they may see your good works, and glorify your Father which is in heaven.* Ye shall know them (Christians) by their fruits.† A good tree cannot bring forth evil fruit, neither can a corrupt tree bring forth good fruit.‡ Wherefore by their fruits ye shall know them.§

When a man equipped with the gifts of the Holy Spirit, like the apostle Paul, writes:

> "Though I speak with the tongues of men and of angels [...] and though I have all faith, so that I could remove mountains [...] and have not charity, it profiteth me nothing."
>
> (1 Corinthians 13:1–3)

then this confession can only elevate the apostle in our veneration, and it has a deep sense when spoken of and to Christians who were blessed with the gifts of the Holy Spirit. To the

---

* [Tr.: Matthew 5:16.]
† [Tr.: Matthew 7:16.]
‡ [Tr.: Matthew 7:18.]
§ [Tr.: Matthew 7:20.]

extent, however, that our present-day theology wants to provide proof thereby that these gifts and works of the spirit are no longer necessary at all these days, that is just sophistry to conceal and gloss over our nakedness, our shame, our poverty, and our blindness.

There, where the living faith already exists, the emphasis must admittedly be placed on the "*love*". But where the faith should first be awoken, the sensually visible persuasion is indispensable. Even Paul himself delivers the most striking evidence for this. He was a contemporary of Christ. To him the glorious deeds of Christ could not have been unfamiliar. Notwithstanding he persecuted in his blindness the body of followers of the holy man. Then all of a sudden the divine light of truth smashed his fanatical zeal, his supposed wisdom. The dark night of his blindness was the sensory persuasion on which his faith ignited and grew stronger. Without this miracle he would have continued his terrible deeds with calm conscience for the honour of God.

Christ rebuked the orthodox Jews, not because they wanted his omnipotence confirmed — but rather because they did not believe him, although he had legitimised his mission through the most glorious miracles. (John 15:22–24.)

Without that sublime work of the spirit the Christian religion would not have been founded. Without those works the Christian religion cannot have spread, let alone become universal. For where no miracles, no powers of the spirit are possible anymore, there is no inner, no *true* life, and even if the faith were just as easily digestible. Where the gifts of the Holy Spirit have totally vanished, there all nourishment is lacking for the faith; without nourishment, however, this highly sacred need must waste away miserably and finally change into mockery, derision, half-heartedness, and indifference or degenerate into dead empty cold observances.

94. The outer life is subject to an eternal metamorphosis, thus the outer life is composed of affliction, doubt, sorrow, illness, misfortune, weakness, stupidity, hardship, and death.

95. The inner life, however, knows no sorrow, knows nothing of weakness. It spreads for itself and its surroundings nothing but bliss and happiness, hence Christ called out: *Come unto*

me (to the inner life), all ye that labour and are heavy laden, and (I, the inner life) I will give you rest.

96. Thus I want then to show with God's help in the second part by what means you can come to Christ for the inner life, the true genuine life, the highest blissful refreshment, and if this refreshment should even only partly come to one, then this text has not been in vain; indeed if even only one person applies these methods and is thereby rescued from fading away, then the publication of this text might appear justified.

Part 2: The Methods for the Inner Life

97. All humans might become happy, but each has a different idea of happiness, and in their methods for happiness they deviate widely.
98. This difference of views has called forth amongst humans those countless schisms, quarrels, and enmities whose end even amongst the Christian associations is not foreseeable at all.
99. *True happiness is only that which lasts eternally*. Transitory happiness, even if yet so splendid, is only an apparent happiness. Hence the earthly life holds no true happiness, because it has no permanence.
100. *Only the inner life is eternally lasting*, hence only here is true happiness to be found. Let us therefore investigate what methods take us there the quickest and most securely.
101. However, before I speak of the methods which lead to the inner life, I consider it necessary to first recall those methods which partly not at all, partly only indirectly take us there, but nonetheless are seen by many people to be genuine methods. These are:

1. Morals

102. The fulfillment of our duties, as well as the observation of the laws of morality cannot directly awaken any inner life. (Luke 17:9–10.) Morals are only the necessary basis without which humans possess no receptivity for the affects of God's spirit. The fulfillment of our duties brings us earthly advantage and God's blessing. Through the latter the path is certainly prepared for the inner life, but provided that we do not wish, believe, covet, and seek, we cannot achieve the true happiness.
103. The claim that the faithful fulfillment of our public duties provides the candidacy to the realm of God, and that God must reward us quite especially on the other side if we loved our spouse in the here and now, fed and raised the children properly, lived chastely and demurely, stood by our neigh-

bour in hardship and grief, obeyed the authorities, fulfilled our offices and business diligently and conscientiously, etc., this claim demonstrates to us the arrogance of a vain self-righteousness and robs us thereby again of the blessing of God which is usually always to be found in the company of simplicity and humility. Even domestic animals must fulfill their public duties. Who makes a fuss then?

104. It is indeed true that by virtue of the eternal righteousness of God everything must be balanced; only the moral way of life is already rewarding in the here and now. — Anyone who loves their wife or their husband is rewarded by returned love. — Anyone who raises their children conscientiously will experience joy in them. — Anyone who is diligent and thrifty will preserves themselves from lack. — Anyone who lives chastely and in moderation will preserve the highest earthly good, their health. — Anyone who obeys the laws of the land also enjoys the benefits of them, etc. But anyone who must nevertheless suffer innocently for a short time, to them their clear conscience is reward for their fidelity. — But those for whom that is no compensation for it, they just have no clear conscience at all, and they will find then their equalisation in the satisfied vanity of their supposed innocence.

105. Those are the external reasons for why fulfilled public duties do not draw the inner life by necessity after them. The inner reasons are yet more convincing: the moral way of life is earthly seed and can therefore bring forth no spiritual fruits, but rather only earthly fruits. — How could love for one's spouse, raising children, diligence, thrift, moderation, chastity, obedience to the authorities, etc., honest virtues which are already socially necessary for our welfare in the here and now, produce a new purer connection, a spiritual body, *the inner life*?! These virtues could, provided that true humility were allied to them, make humans receptive for the spiritual seed from which the inner life should germinate, but fulfilled public duties and morals do not directly draw the inner life after them.

106. I do not want with that to belittle the worth of a moral way of life; but it is possible that someone does not arrive at the inner life despite it (Mark 10:17–23), and on the other hand it is not impossible that even immoral persons awaken

the inner life and thereby obtain the kingdom of heaven, i.e. an eternally happy existence. Matthew 21:31.

107. A second method which is often so rightly considered to be the actual key to the inner life, but produces the inner life as little as the morals, is:

2. Learnedness

All learnedness which needs memory for its existence is earthly, of transitory nature, and can not produce the eternal, the unchanging. — One person may learn the Bible off by heart, another person may have studied all the classics, the old and the new, but the inner life is not produced thereby.

108. The spirit does not need our learnedness, for all knowledge indeed stems from the spirit. (See §§ 31, 43, 44.) Can it please it when we quench our thirst with the runoff of a pond and consider it, the pure crystalline spring which we bear within us, not at all worthy of seeking out?! All learnedness is only a filling up of the skin, it does not penetrate into the flesh and blood, let alone the marrow of the bones. Learnedness is a painted fire; who can warm themselves by it when the earthly body falls apart? Learnedness is like a dead tree on which borrowed fruit hang. — What is knowledge worth which lets us in old age again become childish and awkward! — Learnedness, school knowledge, memory junk are all borrowed wings which we stick on ourselves so that we can flaunt them before other people and would like with them to make ourselves and others believe that we are thereby raising ourselves to heaven, whereas we do not rise a single inch from the earth.

109. No science can raise itself above the domain of the five senses, hence all knowledge, even if it sounds so spiritual, is of an earthly transitory nature. Reason makes conclusions to be sure and produces thereby seemingly purely spiritual products. The premises, however, are based on views, perceptions, and ideas of the five senses, hence the seemingly purely spiritual structure is of earthly origin and therefore cannot ripen from earthly seeds the divine fruit of an eternally happy life. —

110. Notwithstanding the confusion goes so far that many think our learnedness, Luke 10:21, Matthew 5:3 — 5:20, our arts and sciences, John 14:17, that is already inner life! — And

so all powers are incited in order to — live quite sensually with great refinement. Matthew 6:19–20. That is the kingdom of the world, of eternal progress! Every new invention and improvement in trade and commerce is a step towards supposed perfection, and on these steps humanity kneels down to worship the wonders of the world. John 5:43. Revelations 13:8. — With all this apparent greatness, however, poverty and illness, sorrow and misery, discord and disaster, vice and horrors of all sorts are not to be banished from the kingdom of the world, Matthew 22:7, and our statesmen, our scholars and dignitaries of the church wrack their heads in vain over by what methods the demoralisation which goes hand in hand with increasing civilisation could be influenced.

111. If learnedness were the key to the inner life, to the spiritual nature of humanity, then those millions of people who themselves had to do without the most meagre school teaching, who were not in a position to attend colleges and universities, would be greatly lamented. Then the highest good would be the privilege of the individuals, the few; and the majority of all nations, particularly the poor and impecunious, the farmers and craftsmen would be predestined to night and barbarism. — No, such disconsolate views are not to be united with the idea of an all-righteous, all-loving God and Father of all humanity; still less does it stand in harmony with my principle III, by which every human carries the highest knowledge within themselves (§§ 31, 43, 44), hence it is not necessary to beg others, to chew again what others put aside for him, but rather just to seek confidently in himself, to look within himself, to enquire within himself, to knock at his own door — in short, he may go within himself to locate the source from which truth, bliss, and blessedness springs without stop and incessantly. —

112. Humans need only learn to speak with their own spirit, then they will possess the infallible teacher and need not fear being deceived or betrayed. John 17:22, 16:26–27, 16:13. For the spirit, as a part of God, indeed stands in eternal rapport with God and is therefore alone able to reveal to the human the wisdom and the wonder of God. John 14:10, 12:49. Hence away with the vanity of earthly learnedness. Even this at-

tempt can and must not divert the human from the way of truth. John 17:17.

113. In the spirit lies the ability to recognise everything. Humans must identify with this ability, then all the puzzles and wonder of creation will be solved for them. John 17:3. But those who believe they can replace this all-exploring spirit of life by mechanical rote learning are like that rustic who doffed his hat before a wax figure which represented a king. It is not that which you know which has worth — the ability to know and to recognise is that characteristic which marks us as the image of God.

114. After I have argued thus that neither morals, nor learnedness draw the inner life after them by necessity, I come to a point which may be difficult to digest for many devout souls. — Namely the means of grace of the Christian church, baptism and communion, are certainly also methods for the inner life, though Jesus could only introduce these sacraments as a result of his achieved perfection and greatness. There is yet thus a more general viewpoint from which we must ask:

How did Jesus Christ arrive at the true inner life?

115. To the rationalists who deny the so-called miracle of Christ, this question will be very trivial. To them Christ is only a virtuous man and the other side does not concern them. They calmly wait and see what will and can and may come on the other side of the grave. To them the inner life is on the one hand a pious allegorical poem, on the other hand morals whose necessity they comprehend, and in this direction the question of how Christ arrived at the inner life would be answered by firmness of character, power of will. This answer avoids the question, because you are forced straightaway to ask again: yes, how do you arrive then at a firmness of character and power of will that is capable of blessing enemies, praying for them, and *dying* for them! Which is capable of returning health to the sick, life to the dead! — Rationalism owes the answer to this question.

116. To the orthodox by contrast the question of how Jesus Christ arrived at the inner life may simply seem to be sacrilege. To them Christ is the universal divinity. His miracles, his works are the consequence of his omnipotence, and as heaven

is higher than earth, to the same extent does the nature of Christ tower far above that of all other children of men. John 15:5. — Even this view is erroneous and leads us away from the path of truth.

117. Christ is not the universal divinity. According to principle II (§§ 23 and 26), God is immeasurable and could not thus individualise quantitatively into a spatially bounded body. No, one considers the extent of creation. Already our earth, a small planet, exposes a diversity and wealth of appearance so that the observant and thoughtful human moved by sacred awe sinks down worshipful and silent before the throne of the Almighty. Only the earth is nevertheless just a small element in that planetary system whose centre is the sun. Miracle upon miracle becomes accessible here to the serious researcher. But this family group is again only a little point in outer space. Countless stars, galaxies, and nebulae adorn the firmament and form a *universal field of view*, as I call it, namely a hollow immeasurable sphere whose centre is our solar system and whose periphery is those pale nebulae which (on the other side of the milky way) do not want to resolve into suns anymore in our telescopes. — But again there are infinite such fields of view, these fields of view are countless again, immeasurable like the sand in the sea, like the drops in the ocean — boundless — — — and thus the *original cause* of all things gushes, as a fleeting being without the slightest gap or interruption, from planet to planet, from sun to sun, from star to star, from one galaxy to another, from one field of view to another, without stopping, without end — — — !!!

118. And the spirit which animates and rules this immeasurability, an immeasurability which no human can think, grasp, imagine, opposite which the most daring fantasy slackens — this great spirit shall have been concentrated in a human body and wandered about on earth for thirty years?! — This being shall have been spat on, mocked and crucified by the Jews as the only means to be able to forgive his creatures for their sins?!!! — — —

119. No, anyone who wants to believe and think such a thing may go ahead and do what they like; but they would not expect another despite all laws of thinking to raise a pious delusion to the altar of divine worship.

120. Humans are connections of spirit and body (§ 36). If Christ were a being of a higher sort, then he would have to have possessed another body or another spirit. But he had a human body, for he had human needs. But he could not have had a yet more divine spirit, because God is quantitatively indivisible (§ 23). After Christ awoke the inner life in himself, he was certainly a being of a higher sort, but all humans are called to these heights in that all should seek and awaken the inner life. (John 17:21.) But even the inner life is not the universal divinity, but rather only *qualitatively* one with God. John 10:29.

121. Christ was not the universal divinity. No, he could not be that and also never claimed it. Matthew 19:17. Mark 13:32. When it is written: "For in him dwelleth all the fulness of the Godhead bodily"*, then that refers only to the quality, not to the quantity. — Christ is indeed with respect to quality one with God. John 10:30. Christ is therefore related to God like the light ray to the sun — but with respect to quantity Christ himself confessed that the Father is greater than him. John 14:28.

122. Christ was also not predestined to this oneness, to this true inner life. The temptations are indeed expressly mentioned which he had to withstand, Matthew 4:1–11, Luke 4:13–14; if he would have had to have been victorious, then the temptation would indeed have been ridiculous — but if he could succumb to the temptation, then the possibility was indeed present that even he would not achieve the true life, and hence we are justified in asking the question:

How did Jesus Christ arrive at the true inner life?

123. There is no mention of the moral way of life of Christ before his public appearance apart from a too minor matter. It is certainly written that he was subject to his parents, Luke 2:51, only there have at all times been obedient children without the inner life thus being the consequence. Christ must thus have brought yet other methods to use for the obtaining of the inner life.

124. It is the same with learnedness. Christ practised the craftwork of his foster father, he was a carpenter. Mark 6:3. It

---

* [Tr.: Colossians 2:9.]

is not to be thought that as a carpenter he could have been responsible for learning scripture and seeking his wisdom in colleges. This is also confirmed by the astonishing exclamation of the Jews: "How knoweth this man letters, having never learned?" John 7:15 (see § 71).

125. We see from that that morals and learnedness could not have been the seed from which the union with God, i.e. his infallibility, emerged. —

126. After this opening, we will finally be in a place to answer directly the question:

How did Jesus Christ arrive at the true inner life?
And here is the simple answer:
By the practice of letters.

127. This answer requires a comprehensive explanation, to which end it is necessary to envisage the nature of God, which is nothing but **word**, and which is recognised in its power and strength only by letter-thinking.

128. Our first principle (§ 22) was:

There is a cause for all things and we call this original cause "God".

129. If God saw himself caused to create the world, then he must have had a motive for it.

130. But since now there was nothing apart from God, the motive must have lain in him.

131. If it lay in him, then it lay from eternity in him.

132. If it lay from eternity in him, then the world also existed from eternity.

133. If the world existed from eternity, then you must call the whole (*all*) to that extent God, as the attribute of eternity can be attributed only to the divinity (the ***original*** *cause*).

134. Although now the *all* — is *God*, you must though separate the universe into two components, namely into cause and effect or into power and creation.

135. According to that idea, a *power* as the *cause* must have preceded the creation as the effect.

136. Accordingly the essential dignity of divinity is due only to the *power*.

137. The powers of the universe, however, are rooted in the elements of thinking, in the letters, in the language, or, as the holy scripture calls it, in the:

Part 2: The Methods for the Inner Life

"Word"
138. Proof
Elements of thinking = Essence of the powers

139. Thinking encompasses all things which you can imagine.	142. Every power is a sort of movement.
140. Concepts describe the features of ideas.	143. Every movement happens in space and time and is conditioned thereby by matter and form.
141. Absolutely simple thoughts are such whose features and concepts are one (identical).	144. Absolutely simple powers are such in which matter and form are one (identical).

145. This simplicity is possessed by the
letters,
consequently they are
the elements of thinking = the essence of the powers

146. In order for the time being to counter a great misunderstanding, I must note that under "*letters*" as essence of power you are not to understand perhaps the arbitrary signs of various written languages, no, under "*letters*" only the character, the spirit can be meant which lies in the letter-ideas — only the original form can be meant which corresponds to or is identical with the character of these absolutely simple ideas.

147. A few examples will suffice to make this relationship clear and vivid. If you stab, for example, someone suddenly quite finely with a needle tip, he will twitch and cry out in the feeling of pain **I**[*]. — If you by contrast hit someone with a balled fist quite roughly suddenly on the shoulder, he will cry out **U** or **O**. — If in the dark of night a beautiful Bengal light[†] is suddenly ignited, the sight of it usually entices a general **A**. — You will acknowledge that between the character of a needle stab and **I**, between the character of a punch and **O**, and between the character of a Bengal light and **A**, a certain agreement is unmistakeable. — If you examine a small forget-me-not, you cannot think "**U** like charming", but rather only "**I** like charming". — If you by contrast imagine a bear or a

---
* [Tr.: in German, the letter I is pronounced as a long E as in f*ee*l.]
† [Tr.: a type of firework producing a blue flame.]

bull, you cannot as a result think **I** as stocky, as frightful, but rather only **O** as frightful. — With the sight of the sunrise, nobody will be able to cry out anything but **A** as magnificent, not **U** as beautiful.

148. Amongst all the letters, the characters **I A O** stand out the most sharply from one another, so that even the weakest ability to feel and think must acknowledge their omnipotence.

149. As soon as humans dissect the external world in this manner, they finds that they are surrounded by nothing but sheer letters. The word of God is everywhere, God speaks everywhere in the heights and the depths, in solitude and in noise, in heat and frost, in great and small, in near and far, everywhere to which the senses of humans penetrate there is the word of God, there is the *language* of God, and humans have nothing to do but learn to understand, perceive, and feel these letters, these spiritual characters, this living scale, the original forms of the word, **the language powers of God**, in order to infallibly achieve their life goal.

150. The animating, beneficent, and strengthening effect of the outdoors is felt by everyone whose disposition is not yet entirely dulled by earthly worries, or vehemence, or vain bustling.

151. When the city-dweller is almost starved of inner life through politics, sentimentality, and refined sensuality, through speculation, ambition, and shrewdness, in short through his conceptual life, then his chest becomes constricted. He snaps after simple language powers, like the fish when it is thrown onto dry land. He hurries out into nature. The language powers of nature penetrate into his thirsting disposition, he slurps them in with big gulps. He feels the language of God, but he does not understand it. He is incapable of explaining the powerful impression which the spirit of nature exercises on him. He feels that a spirit lies in nature which speaks omnipotently to him; he feels for this spiritual language a sort of echo in his breast; — he feels that between him and this spirit a relatedness, a certain rapport must lie — since an endless yearning seizes his heart — he would like to know himself to be free from all shackles, he would like to kneel down warm with love and drunk with bliss, and cry out loudly to God, his Father, and say, "Father, do not dismiss

your child from your view — draw me to you — let me recognise you — love you!!!"

152. Cheers to the human when in such moments he recognises the path which he must travel. But oh woe, hardly is the momentary stirring over, than the sensual nature of the human awakens and says, "Now we will just see quickly where we will get something good to eat and drink", and thus he withdraws from his inner life again the spiritual nourishment, he does not comprehend that humans do not live from bread alone, but rather from any word which passes through the mouth of God. Matthew 4:4. He does not comprehend that all of nature is nothing but the mouth of God and that the spirit of nature, language powers, are the word of God which must nourish his inner life.

153. But who has showed humans to place the language powers of nature on the same step as passing the time in the theatre! — Do humans believe nature is something so great only so that they can goggle in idle hours and fritter away their lifetime! No, nature is so magnificent because the inner life should become a true image of God. Not for goggling, not for playful flirtatious passing of the time is nature given to humanity, but rather for the nourishment of their inner lives.

154. The language powers of nature are for the inner life that which the scale is for the musician. The letters are the school for the inner life. Humans must let the spirit of the various characters act on them for as long as until their feeling for life is raised to an infallibility similar to the ear for music, until God stops being something distant and foreign and they can speak with God as with themselves.

155. Every tree, every bush, every flower, every leaf — every mountain, every cliff, every stone, every spring, every star, every sea and lake — the sky and firmament, day and night — summer and winter — snow and rain — zephyr and hurricane — the cold and the heat — thunder and lightning — the hard and the soft — the easy and the difficult — the slow and the quick — in short everything, everything, every form, every colour, every sound, every movement — everything which only the senses perceive has its distinguishable character and these characters are the language powers of God which in the last instance may be reduced to the spirit of the letters, and

this spirit humans must take up within themselves, this spirit humans must learn to feel and experience as letters — then they will be learning to speak with God — then they will be forming their inner life, then they will be awakening Christ within themselves, then they will be becoming a child, a son or daughter, an image of God, and privy to all the spiritual powers which lie in the nature of the divinity.

156. God is the word and the word is letters. How is that to be understood? Think of the beginning of creation. Nowhere there were there worlds, beings, creatures — nothing was present but empty space. This space could not, however, have been entirely empty, otherwise nothing could have originated in it. The space was thus filled with powers, and as far as the space went, as far was it filled by these powers without interruption or gap. There was thus at the beginning nothing but a simple substance, a being, a power, call it what you will, in short a something which filled space. — Now if this being wanted to do something, make something, then it had to be active. Every activity, however, is a movement. But every movement is a form. — Every movement has its specific character. The simplest forms, the simplest characters, consequently the simplest movements are the letters. Therefore as soon as God is active, he speaks. His activity is his language and the language is the nature or the name of God.

157. When in the story of creation it is written: "And God said, Let there be light: and there was light"*, then you must not thus imagine that God expressed this command like a human, at which suddenly in an inexplicable way light originated. No, that idea would be a silly one. We would thereby place the divinity in the category of sorcerers and transform his word into an arbitrary use of power, against which the most extreme fantasies of a person suffering from fever would be in conformity with natural law. No, when God spoke, there was light, which means as much as that the language elements, the word, the power of the universe moved, formed for all light particles of the ether a point of attraction, gathered them up into luminous fiery spheres and placed them as suns up in the heavens. This activity of God cannot have been described

---

* [Tr.: Genesis 1:3.]

more fittingly than by the expression, "God *spoke*, it became light", to the extent every act of creation is an activity — every activity a movement — every movement a form and every form is a letter. From the letters, however, words form, and hence the creative power of God is called his language or his name.

158. Language serves humans in order to form concepts from it, whereby they share their thoughts with each other. — This form of use is only a less important feature of language. Its true, but unfortunately almost entirely unknown worth rests in its *strength*.

159. Language as *power* is the name of God which shall be considered sacred, and if in Revelations 1:8 and 22:13 Jesus says of himself (of the inner life), "I am Alpha and Omega*", he thus says thereby, *I am the entire alphabet.*

160. Father, word, and spirit are the eternal inviolable trinity of God, as it stands written: For there are three that bear record in heaven, the Father, the Word, and the Holy Ghost: and these three are one. 1 John 5:7.

161. The Father is the being at large in space who is present everywhere.

162. The word is the power of the Father, and this power consists of the letters whose fusion and alteration produces the riches of creation, never repeating itself, ever again different, and yet eternally the same.

163. The character of the letters, however, is the spirit which individualises itself through the word, everywhere an allegory of God. The spirit is the mouth of God which trumpets the omnipotence and greatness and wonder of God with thunderous voice — oh if the human race could hear this thunderous voice!

164. The Father is the primary matter, the original element, the original cause, and this primary material is nothing but pure power.

165. The Son is the movement of this power, the activity of these powers or the word because every movement consists of letters.

---

*   [Tr.: alpha and omega = Greek A and O. A being the first letter of the ancient Greek alphabet, and O being the last.]

166. The spirit, however, is the specific character of these movements, and humans must learn to feel and experience, perceive and understand these characters in all the parts of their body; then they will be learning to speak with God, then they will be becoming illuminated ones for whom every puzzle solves itself and who are thereby being raised up to the highest virtue, to the love of God.

167. God or primary matter or *original cause* as *power* — *Son* or *word* as movement of these powers — and *spirit* as peculiarity of the power or character of the movement — these three are one, were one, and will in all eternity remain one. Whether it is recognised or not by humans blinded by orthodoxy or rationalism or enraptured in sensuality, it does not change one iota the laws of eternity.

168. The chemists call gold, iron, platinum, hydrogen, carbon, oxygen, etc. — simple bodies — why? Because no method is known to them of dismembering these bodies into yet simpler components. With that they document probably the boundaries of the art of their analytical laboratories, but the thinker cannot be concerned with technical expressions. The thinker has no need of asking after how far the earthly human has made the powers of visible nature accessible to himself. Does chemistry also have a method for smelting coal, for freezing ethyl alcohol, or forming organic bodies?!

169. Chemistry with its limited aids may not be able to separate out the components of gold in reality — but the thinker can do it in the idea.

170. Gold is yellow, heavy, hard, malleable, elastic, porous, and has numerous chemical properties. But now the weight, colour, hardness, malleability, etc. are not gold, how can gold thus be a simple body!!! If the thinker distances from gold in the idea all the characteristics, what remains in the end of the gold?!

171. I call in contrast upon all the thinkers of the entire world to separate the thoughts I, A, O, U, M, P, R, K, etc., in short

Part 2: The Methods for the Inner Life

the 9 vowels* and the 16 consonants† into yet simpler components!

172. Here there is stability, here there is the real presence of God. — Whereas all the matter of the entire world is subject to eternal change — the letters do not change. The entire universe might even be reduced to ruins and transform into a new chaos, the letters will remain eternally that which they were, which they are, and which they will be.

173. After we have now consequently discovered a spiritual potency, a being, a spiritual matter which never changes, which never dies, which can never go to ruin, we have also discovered the method from which and by which a new, spiritual, indestructible body can be formed. 1 Corinthians 15:46.

174. Through the elements of thinking humans possess the key to the inner life, to the knowledge of all things, to the powers of all creation — to the highest perfection, infallibility — union with God.

175. God has given himself to humanity, for the spirit of a human is a part of God. But still more, he has through the language of letters lent humanity the ability to get to know this spirit in its strength and to identify the ego with this strength.

176. Now how does that happen? When the human is born, he learns first of all to stand upright, to walk, and to speak. The consciousness animates itself through the external language. It develops understanding, reason, and will. Now just as the outer human learnt to want, think, and feel through oral language, the spiritual human must now learn to want, think, and feel within through the language of thoughts or through the thought language. But just as the child must first learn to stand and walk, so the human, if he wants to obtain the inner life, if he wants to become independent, must first learn to think and feel letters at the foundation in the feet.

177. This practice of letters is the *original religion*, is the universal law of life without which neither a knowledge of God, nor self-knowledge, nor cognition of the truth, nor an inner

---

* [Tr.: in the German, the 9 vowels referred to are most likely A, E, I, O, U, Ä, Ö, Ü, Y.]

† [Tr.: this number works if you treat voiced and unvoiced as equivalent, etc. — i.e. C/K = G, B = P, D = T — and separate Q into its components: K+W.]

life, nor the rebirth, nor an eternally lasting happiness is ever possible.

178. As soon as the human is seven years old, he must dedicate himself daily for an hour exclusively to this business, this activity. This activity in and of itself is as easy as child's play, you must do no more than stand upright, speak the letters *in your mind*, and move your ego into your feet. The exercise is easy, but for persistence and stamina the entire energy of which a human is capable is necessary.

179. As long as this letter practice is not preached in the churches, is not taught to the children in school, and it is neglected to use this method in all life tasks to produce the inner life in oneself, for just as long will Christianity remain at the pitiful stage at which it has found itself since the time when paganism turned en masse through the orders of the Roman emperor with all the horrors of the degenerate church service into a mouthed Christianity.

180. The practice of letters is the universal law of life which is to be brought into use in all the tasks of life.

181. If the human rises early, then he should think the letters into himself as he gets dressed.

182. The farmer must now go into his stalls in order to feed and groom his animals. This work demands so little thought that he at the same time can quite comfortably think letters in his feet.

183. He now goes out into the field and sows, or ploughs, or harvests. He can at the same time quite well speak letters in thought and endeavour to learn to feel them in his feet.

184. The craftsman can almost always, despite plying his trade, be practising letters in his feet.

185. The smith, the metalworker, when they are hammering on the anvil, or filing, can at the same time learn to think letters in their feet.

186. The tailor, the cobbler can with their work quite well speak letters in their feet.

187. The soldier, when he is standing at his sentry post, can do nothing better than use this time in order to practise letters in his feet in a beautifully upright pose.

Part 2: The Methods for the Inner Life

The factory worker who lingers thoughtlessly by his machine and exercises mechanically his few tasks can at the same time learn to feel letters in his feet.

188. An invalid who is restricted to his bed and feels boredom can do nothing better for his bodily and spiritual health than think uninterruptedly letters in himself and learn to feel them in the feet.

189. The female gender can indeed almost practise thinking letters into themselves in every life task and by virtue of their delicate nerve structure they are able much more easily and nimbly to feel the letters in their feet. Young ladies of noble descent in particular would learn the matter in a fabulously short time, and if this practice of letters is ever taught in general, then amongst the mentioned young ladies the prophetesses will grow like mushrooms from the earth.

190. The merchants and scholars come off worst of all. These cannot with their professional business think letters because their thought power is taken up in any case. But all will also not be in vain: the last shall be first, and the first last.*

191. These must absolutely sacrifice an hour a day in order to dedicate themselves to the activity of the letters. To anyone for whom that seems unworkable, consider that as soon as humans seize on a wish with full desire, they know how to always spare enough time for its realisation. Anyone who has previously slept 8 hours, they now sleep 7 hours. Anyone who previously spent two hours in the tavern, they now let one hour suffice, and so on. There is no greater foolishness than when the businessman says he has no time for himself because of all the work. Anyone who does not have time for themselves, they also do not have time for their home, and who then wants to stray eternally in strange lands, strive and torment themselves with strangers, without reward, without thanks, whereas he can live at home enjoying himself and in peace. Scholars usually have more free time. Our country pastors often do not know at all how they should spend their time. Might they though speak thoughtfully into their feet the word of life for as long as until the inner life ignites itself and they have found for the *written* word of God the right com-

---

*   [Tr.: Matthew 20:16.]

mentary — the right interpreter, the *living* word of God in themselves.

192. Precisely our educated classes might consider that if they only ever use the purely spiritual potencies of wanting, thinking, and feeling in order to fulfill their earthly profession, then they will belong amongst the number of those who bury the pound entrusted to them in the earth*, i.e. in the earthly. By wanting, thinking, and feeling, humans must also awaken and nourish their inner spiritual life, and that is only possible through letter work.

193. The letter practice is accessible to all. No class, no stature, no religion, no language, no stage of education is excluded from it.

194. The miner when he is spending his miserable existence in hard work down in the shaft underground, he can at the same time be working with letters, he should awaken the inner life in his feet and thereby reveal the prospect of a happy life.

195. The criminal who serves his sentence in a solitary cell can do nothing better at all than think the alphabet into his feet without interruption in order to be blessed with the promise: "though your sins be as scarlet, they shall be [made] as white as snow [by the inner life]". Isaiah 1:18.

196. For those people whose profession involves living in isolated regions or who are much alone in isolated regions, the inner life often arrives as if headed for them.

197. We have already seen above (§§ 149–155) that all that the senses perceive are language elements of the word of God. These language powers work incessantly and penetrate productively into the disposition of humans. — Now for those who are thus often alone, like e.g. hunters, shepherds, mariners, etc., the language powers of the nature surrounding them affect them far more powerfully because their ideas are not as occupied by the events of the world as is the case with city dwellers.

198. Only here accident reigns still, and as wonderful too as the phenomena of the inner life are which you come across in this class of humans, humans though must not leave their

---

* [Tr.: cf. Matthew 25:14–30.]

greatest good to accident. They can and should also be using external nature, but since they can through the power of thought make their own the simplest language powers of the living word of God,

letter work

remains the foundation law of life.

199. In order to be able to devote themselves to this activity constantly, at the beginning of the Christian era the hermits and later the monasteries arose. — The inner life to a high perfection was sometimes the fruit of persistent activity. As a result they established the reputation for especial holiness. You went to them when you needed advice and comfort. The comforted returned home with joyous heart, and sought by charitable gifts to show their gratitude. Then the monasteries by and by became rich, and the wealth led to their degeneration, their ruin. The actual goal — development of the inner life — was forgotten, and haughtiness, vanity, inordinate ambition, luxury, in short sensuality then celebrated the same triumph as before.

200. Humans must not isolate themselves. Humans can achieve the highest perfection only amongst humanity. Any isolation makes them one-sided and robs them of the purely human virtues, love, forbearance, patience, pity, and charity, without which the inner life is only a ringing bell, a resounding bronze. Christ did not isolate himself. He lived amongst humanity and earned his daily bread by handwork like any other. He did not go out of the way of the temptations of life, but vanquished them. Woe to the human race if loneliness were required for the awakening of the inner life. How many would then like to obtain it, and if everyone isolated themselves, what then should become of society?

201. To entirely separate from your fellow humans and to not separate at all from your business, plans, and earthly delights; to be always alone and to never go into oneself, both directions are wrong, lead to going astray, and produce harmful consequences.

202. For that reason, amongst all religious orders Free Masonry is the most reasonable. It alone lets humans exist amongst their like in all their external relationships as they are, urges by contrast incessantly for the awakening of the in-

ner life and shows them by the nature of the matter the most certain and simplest method.

203. Humans should daily spend an hour on nourishment and awakening of the inner life by betaking themselves into *isolation* and learning to experience in their feet the spirit of the letters. — For the rest no isolation is needed, can indeed become harmful and does not lie in the plan of the creator.

204. What the breath is for the earthly body, letter work is for the spiritual body. Humans must make themselves capable of being able to breathe in and out thinking letters in all organs and parts of their bodies, then they will be dining on divine immortal manna from which eternal life flows; for the nature of letters is nothing but pure power and strength.

205. Mere brooding, arguing, and opining is of no help here. Humans must apply themselves to the work, and when one has exercised for thirty years daily in thinking the letters, then he will have become fully aware of what sort of character the strength of the letters has. — Through shrewdness, however, humans will never obtain knowledge of the strength which lies in them — but rather they can through activity.

206. The Holy Trinity of Father, word, and spirit finds in humans its parallel via the three potencies: wanting, thinking, and feeling.

207. Just as Father, word, and spirit are one, so are wanting, thinking, and feeling one. — For nobody can want without thinking and feeling. Nobody can think without wanting and feeling. Nobody can feel, be conscious of themselves, without wanting and thinking.

208. If humans want to achieve the greatest good, it can only happen through the activity of these three potencies.

209. All the laws of earthly and spiritual nature teach that like can only produce like (Luke 11:17). Water cannot dry, fire cannot make cold. Hate cannot produce love, etc.

210. The *will* of God is absolute freedom.

211. True happiness is only thinkable with absolute freedom.

212. Free is that which you can neither command, nor forbid, that which is compelled or hindered by neither inner, nor outer force.

213. These conditions are fulfilled in the letter-thinking. No force can command or forbid it, can compel or prevent it.

Here is the seed from which the true happiness of absolute freedom can sprout.

214. Humans must make use of free methods to achieve the *highest*, because it can on the one hand only be achieved by *free* methods, and because on the other hand it is just as shameful as ridiculous to strive for the noble and sublime by unfree methods. Woe to the human race if the acquiring of the inner life were absolutely bound to giving alms, fasting, attending church, school education, baptism, communion, and the like to which you can force a human or away from which you can hold a human. What sort of happiness would that be to which the possibility of forcing a human to it was not excluded!!! Is that not a contradiction — nonsense. — Or what sort of world order would it be if the highest, indeed only true good could be withheld!

215. As it is with wanting, so it is with thinking. Accordingly the question must be answered:

"What is thinking?"

and we will straightaway see that the correct definition of thinking contains the same key to the inner life.

216. Since humans are not independent powers and beings, but rather according to principle **III** a combination of spirit and body, they can only learn thinking from the spirit. We must therefore first answer the question:

How does the spirit think?

217. The thinking of the spirit consists, however, as we have already seen above (§§ 136–145) in its activity. Its activity reveals itself in its movements. All movements have a character, and the simplest characters are the letters. Consequently the letters are the elements of thinking.

218. The spirit therefore does not learn thinking, but rather its being is the thinking power, i.e. the original forms of its movements are identical with the elements of thinking.

219. Now if thus, for example, the **I** represents the inner, midmost, fine, sharp, charming, reflective, etc.; the **A** the sublime, magnificent; the **Ae** the pitiful; the **R** the shocking, thundering, swirling, trembling; the **P T K** the pushing, knocking, hammering; the **W L CH** the wafting, breathing; the **M N nG** the pressing, the heavy, etc., then learning to think means nothing more for humans than getting to know

the various characteristics of these spiritual movements. This getting to know can only happen through humans thinking themselves into the letters for so long until they become (a spiritual) flesh and blood in them, i.e. until they feel and experience the spirit of the letters in all parts of their body clearly and distinctly.

220. With all educated peoples of the ancient world, this doctrine formed the core of the religious mysteries, is hinted at in its abstract purity still today in the rituals of freemasonry, and is, as I will later show, expressed in the four gospels on every page, but always with that brevity, acuity, and conciseness that has become the enigmatic sphinx of our leisurely thought and resembles the flaming sword with which the cherub guards the entrance to paradise.

221. A matter which can find a concise explanation through the correct definition of thinking is the so-called "occurring".

222. When we do not know something and yet would like to get clear about it, we think about it, and if we are persistent in our thinking about it, then we often suddenly find the sought for, and we then say the thought *occurred* to us.

223. Since thinking means so much as to feel the movements of the spirit, the actual thinking does not only consist of us imagining an object, but rather also *feeling* this idea in our inner being, i.e. we become conscious of the impression which an idea makes on the spirit. Now *the* difference between knowing and not knowing is that in one case we arrive at consciousness of this impression, and in the other case do not. An example will make that clear: I put sugar on my tongue. Now as soon as I become conscious of the impression which the sugar makes on my tongue, I say the sugar is sweet. — From this you see that the actual knowing can be taught to nobody. Nobody can explain how bananas taste. Anyone who has already tasted this fruit knows it — the others do not, and no learnedness is capable of explaining the matter to them. As in the earthly, so in the spiritual. Anyone who has already loved knows what love is, but it cannot be explained. It stands likewise with God. Anyone who experiences the spirit of the letters knows what God is. But it cannot be explained, and there is therefore no other advice in heaven and on earth than that each shall think the letters into themselves for so long as

until they are conscious of the impression which they make on the spirit, then they will know what God is, and not sooner.

224. Knowing accordingly has three stages:

225. 1) *Imagining*.

The object (the objective word) touches the sense. The nerves bring the touch to the brain and receives from there the response, the echo, the answer, and this answer returns again to the sense, and then the sensation is complete.

226. 2) *Speaking*.

The complete sensation passes again through the body and touches the spirit for the second time. The spirit moves then in accordance with the touch through its original forms, through the letters, and forms a word which is homogeneous to the sensation, and through this speaking the complete sensation becomes for the human a *clear thought*.

227. You see from this what a forceful difference there is between an original language and a bastard language.

228. Think of a prehistoric man. He is in full possession of innocence. His feeling is pure, unadulterated, preoccupied by nothing. No prejudices, superstitions, or preconceived notions darken his disposition. His wanting, thinking, and feeling are alive in him. Now the language powers of nature penetrate through the senses into *him*, and find in him a lively echo. What God speaks into him through nature — that speaks out from him again. He sucks the air into himself, he *breathes*, he *respires*; the finest of all bodies, the *light*, penetrates into his eyes. He hears the *rustling* of the trees, the *thunder* and *lightning* of the *storm*, he sees the *bubbling* of the *spring*, etc. Now he will name all these objects in conformance with the impression they make on his disposition. If you compare the objects with the character of the following words: thunder, lightning, crash, rumble, hard, weak, sweet, sour, bitter, tart, mild, meek, love, rage, vengeance, hate, angst, grumble, drone, splinter, rush, etc., then you fill find how in the spirit the letters express the nature of the things themselves. — A bastard language will dispense with this peculiarity to the degree that the base sounds of the original language from which it originated have blurred. When the French speak of love, so it is suggested, an ox bellows.

229. Since now of all the educated nations the Germans alone possess a cultivated language, the Germans must become the lords of the world as soon as they recognise the power which lies in their language.

230. Thinking is therefore nothing more than the endeavour of grabbing the impression or becoming conscious of the impression which a question makes on the spirit, and as soon as we succeed in experiencing this impression, we have the other word, the answer, (the subjective word) and then say the thought has occurred to us.

231. You see from that how much for the novice it depends on the adroit formulation of the question, and for anyone who does not become weary with thinking, changing the formulation of the question again and again, everything they wish must finally occur to them, assuming that they have not neglected to produce in themselves and cultivate those spiritual organs or tools by means of which you can measure the finest oscillations in the activity of the spirit, as it then stands written: "the Spirit searcheth all things, yea, the deep things of God." 1 Corinthians 2:10.

232. In the Kabbalah it hence stands written: Someone who can count to fifty is a complete man. The Kabbalah thus divides humans into 7 octaves, as follows: foot, leg, thigh, belly, chest, neck, head. When you divide each octave again into seven tones, then the human body is a keyboard of 49 tones. Now anyone who can count up to 50 parts in which they can think and feel letters, i.e. is conscious of their spiritual powers, they are a complete man.

233. The Delphic oracle declared Socrates to be the wisest of men because he avowed of himself, "he knows nothing." This confession is not to be understood to the effect of Socrates realising his ignorance — but rather the emphasis lies on the "he". He, Socrates, the human, the connection knew nothing, his knowing arose all from the spirit, from the inner life. Socrates was one of those few who recognised that the human has no knowledge of his own, but rather that our knowledge is only a reflection. As the moon possesses only the reflection of the sun as light — so too is our knowledge only a reflection of the spiritual powers within us, and on this basis Socrates said of himself that "he" knew nothing.

234. The third stage of knowing is finally (see §§ 225 and 226):
  3) *Feeling*.
The clear thought passes for the third time through the body and experiences itself (the subjective word) and thereby comes alive (as substance).

235. With this at the same time the activity of the third potency of feeling is expressed (see §§ 206–208).

236. The ideas and the power of ideas (word) are not a mere nothing, a something which dispenses with reality! Spirit is not an insubstantial being — no, on the contrary, the spirit is the only real body, the only real substance, and becomes individual as soon as the human learns to feel, to experience these powers.

237. There are no absolute opposites.

238. God is the only true real something. If there were absolute opposites, then there would also have to be a "*nothing*", there would have to be a something which would be nothing, which is nonsense.

239. Hence when a human thinks **I**, then this thought is not perhaps a nothing, but rather this thought is a real substantial something, and if the corporeality of the thoughts **I, A, O**, etc. were so fine that the light of the sun would be coarse, rough material in contrast, then the thinker can never concede that the spirit and its thoughts are absolutely incorporeal, simply because there are no *absolute* opposites. 1 Corinthians 15:40.

240. But if there are no absolute opposites, then between body and spirit, between body and power there is also only relative difference.

241. The body is a coarse spirit and the spirit is a fine body. The body is a rough power and the power a purified body.

If nonetheless you therefore only comprehend under "body" that which is perceived with the five senses, then with that the corporeal world is not yet exhausted. There are still finer senses which perceive a new, a spiritual corporeal world. Proof for that are dreams, whereby senses open themselves, are capable of perceiving the thought objects physically. — Proof for that is the text in the Bible: "Blessed are the pure in heart: for they shall see God."[*] In pure hearts an eye forms which is capable of perceiving the highest purity. God, the spiritual being contrasted with the corporeal world, is with respect to his nature not simply all corporeality, simply because he can be seen by pure hearts.

242. The nature of all things can only be distinguished in its temper or, as the chemists say, in its aggregate state.

Only you must not limit these states to the three chemical ones, but rather extend them to the seven universal aggregate states, namely to:

"fixed, fluid, airy, etheric, vegetable, living, spiritual".

In these states is contained everything humans can think, suspect, and believe.

243. Now you will also recognise what wants to be said: "to learn to feel the thoughts, i.e. to make substantial." When humans absorb an idea into themselves and occupy themselves with it over and over again, it becomes intrinsically substantial within them. It forms a sort of rebirth, a new spiritual being which is homogeneous to the idea, which is the idea become flesh into which the ego of the human passes, indeed so that the human in the end cannot want, think, and feel at all anymore other than by bringing the nature of this idea become flesh along.

244. This rebirth requires much effort, diligence, persistence. The new being is not finished straightaway.

245. The first beginning is the zeal and the desire from which in the end life develops as far as enthusiasm. The most difficult thing then becomes easy for humans, they vanquish all obstacles, for it is not them who works and creates there, but rather the divine language power coming to life and gaining consciousness within them.

246. This law remains for good or worse the same, in just things as in wrong things, as it stands written: With the merciful thou wilt shew thyself merciful; with an upright man thou wilt shew thyself upright; With the pure thou wilt shew thyself pure; and with the froward thou wilt shew thyself froward. Psalm 18:25–26.

---

[*] [Tr.: Matthew 5:8.]

247. Anyone who thus, for example, devotes themselves to the idea of haughtiness and renders homage to this idea over and over again, in this human this idea becomes in the end substantial, intrinsic, and we then say that he is possessed by a fixed idea. This fixed idea is a sort of rebirth, is a demonic being within him, is a deformity of the inner life which now, like all that is alive in the world, desires sustenance, and provided that the external world offers no such sustenance, at least seeks and finds in the idea satisfaction of his needs. — Such a one considers stools and benches to be his subjects, thinks himself to be a great lord, and we call him a fool.

248. Here the path of nature is written with symbols of flame. What humans sow, they will reap*. Anyone who sows on the spirit will reap from the spirit eternal life, but anyone who sows on the flesh will reap from the flesh ruin†.

249. All the ideas which humans take up into themselves are creative powers.

250. That this is really the case, we see already in the earthly state in the so-called birthmarks, e.g. a pregnant woman sees a mouse leap across the path towards her — she grasps her leg in shock and the new-born child has a mouse fur on its leg. — Another woman has a cherry thrown at her ear — she is startled and the child has a clump of flesh like a cherry hanging from its ear. — A poor pregnant woman gets a craving for sausage — she is too poor to satisfy her craving — she gives birth and the child has a sausage lying on its cheeks.

251. The more exclusively do humans devote themselves to some idea, the more specifically one-sided their inner life will turn out.

252. The one person chases after honour, the other after money, the third after beauty, the fourth after power. These ideas bring about a sort of rebirth. As soon as the earthly body breaks up, the inner life is left there as a deformity and desires sustenance. — But now how will the haughty, the miserly, the overambitious find satisfaction on the other side? Thus they must perish and slowly starve until the connection dissolves again and all the material returns into its elements.

---

* [Tr.: cf. Galatians 6:7.]
† [Tr.: cf. Galatians 6:8.]

253. What now should humans do? They should not bring to life this or that idea in themselves, but rather should bring to life in themselves the root of all ideas, the language powers of God, the three-fold sacred names of God, the *letters*. The spirit of the letters is neither good, nor bad, just like the will which as absolute freedom also knows no good and evil anymore.

254. As we have seen above, the letters are the name of God because the characters of all powers or movements are simplified into the letters.

255. All movements though can be seen as variations of a three-fold basic theme, or amongst all movements there are three which express their character most sharply, namely the line, the angle, and the circle. But since in the disposition the line expresses itself constantly as an **I**, the angle constantly as an **A**, and the circle constantly as an **O**, thus **I A O** is the root of the name of God.

256. We again find this root name in the mysteries of all the religions.

257. With the Jews, it is found in the names of the three patriarchs: Abraham, Isaac, and Jacob. Jews should therefore first bring to life in themselves the **A**, then add to it the **I**, then finally the **O**. Abraham, Isaac, and Jacob speak with God. In these three names Jews were also able to learn to speak with God, i.e. if through these three names they brought to life in themselves the root name of God, then they felt the movements of the language powers of God = they spoke with God.

258. The same root is found in the sacred name of God, Jehovah. The actual name was a long time ago certainly Ieoua, i.e. five vowels as five life streams. The Jews shall have constantly *thought* these life streams into themselves, for it was forbidden as desecration to speak it out loud.

259. The vowels are the life streams, the consonants the incisions for individualisation.

260. The root of the name of God is found again in the forerunner of Christ, John, who was thus named according to the express command of God — why? In order to characterise the symbolic interpretation of Christ, i.e. the inner life, also in this direction. Firstly humans must feel and experience in

themselves **I O A**, before Christ, the full inner life, can set root and arrive at the fullest maturity.

261. Christ finally handed over this root to his believers again in Simon. He called him at first Peter and said: And I say also unto thee, That thou art Peter, and upon this rock I will build my church; and the gates of hell shall not prevail against it.[*] Before his ascension he gave Simon also the name Jonah, the root of the name of God. (John 21:15–17[†].) — Peter shall thus have first learned to feel in himself **E U**[‡] and then **I O A**. These vowels again form the ancient name of God **I E O U A** and on this rock the Church of Christ remains standing.

262. After these discussions of the letter practice as the sole method for the true inner life, we may be in a position to understand those texts of the New Testament and in particular of the four gospels which concern the inner life and the methods for it. I have collated these references in sacred scripture for the theory of life in a special section.

---

[*] [Tr.: Matthew 16:18.]
[†] [Tr.: in this text in Luther's 1545 German Bible, Jesus addresses Simon as Simon Jona. In the King James Version he is addressed as Simon, son of Jonas. Most other versions, both German and English, translate it as Simon, son of Jonas/Jonah/John.]
[‡] [Tr.: i.e. **Petrus** (Latin for Peter).]

Part 3: The Evidence of Sacred Scripture

263. Sacred scripture has no other aim at all but to give humans a proper idea of the inner life, to awaken the faith in it, to spur them on to seek it, and finally to provide the best methods for achieving it.

264. For anyone of uninhibited heart who seeks in it, the true understanding must unlock itself bit by bit; but anyone who wants at no price to let go of their preconceived opinions must certainly recognise in it everywhere puzzles and miracles, or legends and folk tales.

265. That the four gospels, which barely take up the space of four printed sheets, have not yet found any generally accepted explanation in the space of eighteen centuries is an irreconcilable pity and shame for the entirety of Christendom.

266. If Christianity wants to establish a confession of faith, then that can only be drawn from the four gospels, because the letters can well be explained by the gospels, but not vice versa. The epistles cannot contain anything new and would be inexplicable without the gospels. — Not so, however, for the gospels. In them, the life, works, nature, and the doctrine of Christ is contained entirely and can be neither completed nor clarified by the epistles. I do not want with that to belittle the worth of the epistles, I am just protesting against making them the basis of a confession of faith; for the letters are lacking here the necessary generality. The letters bear the stamp of the personality of the writer and were specifically intended for the state of the respective congregation. These letters stand in direct connection with the oral teachings of the apostles, and since these oral teachings were not (stenographically) handed down to us, we are lacking in the first instance the necessary context and even if we possessed these (stenographic) reports, the apostles could secondly only have reproduced the pure doctrine and this doctrine is found expressed in its completeness and generality in the four gospels.

267. In the four gospels themselves, the parables of the kingdom of God which Christ puts forward stands paramount. In the parables Christ makes the relationship clear between the here and now and the other side, between the inner and outer life, between the three kingdoms: hell, the world, and heaven. In the parables the foundational law of life is contained and only this original law can be the content of a confession of faith.

268. In all Christ's words there is truth, but only in the parables is the theory of the true life *completely* contained.

269. The parables are the crux of Christianity; in the parables lies the unalterable mathematical point which cannot pass away, even if heaven and earth pass away. The parables contain the original law, the fixed necessity, for they all appeal to the natural laws known to us and remind us that with obtaining the highest good the ways of natural law must be entered on and arbitrariness avoided.

270. If you had from time immemorial only sought the original law contained in all the parables and made this law alone the content of the Christian confession of faith, then the teachings of Christ would have been brought into practice and been exalted by the fruits and works of the spirit and not perished in sophistical disputes, hair-splitting theorems which in themselves becomes accessible to the inner life but remain as eternally incomprehensible to intellectuals and those of the world as the harmony of the tones to the deaf, as the theory of colours to the blind.

271. How shall it help if the child must learn by rote:
"Christ died for our sins."
"Christ was born to the virgin Mary by the Holy Spirit."
"Baptism brings about the forgiveness of sins."
"Bread and wine are the true body of Christ." etc.
Teach the child to seek the inner life, and when it has found the inner life, the life and works of Christ will become clear by themselves, but before that it is as impossible as for the unmusical ear to be able to grasp that the keynote, third, and fifth form a chord.

272. Blinded by pious zeal, we think we are nevertheless advancing Christendom. when we have the child learn by rote these (for them at the time) incomprehensible things and

force it to at least seemingly believe in them. From that now arises on the one hand bigotry and superstition, from that arises opinion and mania which can transform humans into tigers and hyenas where they fancy they have to carry out every horrible deed for the honour of God; on the other hand, however, doubt awakens with maturer age. The doubters shake off from themselves the shackles pushed onto them, they smell fraud, and finally obtain the hair-raising suspicion that all the priests and pastors have conspired against his eternal salvation, that they, in order to dominate him all the more securely and exploit him for the sake of earthly aims, have led him from earliest childhood intentionally and knowingly into deepest night and stupidity, and thus awake in him hate and derision towards an entire corporation, the faith in humanity is carried to the grave, the love for God and humanity must escape from the breast, and the kingdom of God is further from us than ever.

273. The confession of faith of a child simply cannot be enough. Everything which requires just the tiniest bit of acumen for its understanding is not only useless for a child, but harmful. Had I put up a confession of faith for children, it would sound something like:

274. "Through letter thinking the human learns to hear the voice of the holy spirit, and when he hears and follows the word of this spirit he becomes happy."

275. No force in heaven and on earth can lend humans blessedness, provided that they do not make an independent effort for it. But if they must make an independent effort, then teach the children this activity and wait with the depths of Christianity as long as until the living interpreter is born in the child — then the truth will meet in them and they will learn to understand the life and works of Christ by themselves better than it can ever be expressed by the tongues of men.

276. Christ indeed expressly said to his disciples:
> "I have yet many things to say unto you, but ye cannot bear them now." John 16:12.

If the disciples could not after three years of contact with their master grasp the depths of Christian doctrine, about how much less can you bother children with it.

277. And Christ said again: If you do not understand me when I speak of earthly things, how will you understand me when I speak of heavenly things!* From this it emerges again that the earthly sensual human comprehends nothing of the spirit of God — it is therefore not only useless, but is even harmful to want to overstuff a child with it.

278. On the contrary, Christ said to his disciples: Howbeit when he, the Spirit of truth, is come, he will guide you into all truth: for he shall not speak of himself; but whatsoever he shall hear, that shall he speak: and he will shew you things to come. John 16:13.

279. That which the disciples had need of, we have double the need of. The recognition of truth is not a mechanical thing which a human can share with others — but rather a living thing which strikes roots as a feeling of life in the human and finally grows to be a great mighty tree of faith, of knowledge, of awe.

280. You can therefore effectively only make the child familiar with the methods by which it can become a Christian — the nature of Christianity itself must become clear in him through his own activity. Any other mechanically rote-learned confession of faith is a painted fire which provides neither light nor warmth.

281. Returning to the parables of the kingdom of God, a very important circumstance must be noted. The rebirth is namely, as I have already mentioned in my principle **IV** (see § 64), a two-fold one:

    a) a bodily or substantial one,
    b) an ethical or moral one.

All the parables, indeed all the sayings of Christ which refer to the inner life, also have therefore a double meaning, namely a bodily or material, and an ethical or moral meaning.

282. Both meanings must not be confused with one another either, nor even (as up to now happens almost generally) may the bodily, material meaning be ignored.

283. Here is a cliff on which already the best thinkers, the most pious dispositions, indeed the reborn themselves have failed.

---

*   [Tr.: cf. John 3:12.]

284. Always they find in the parables nothing more than morals. You therefore teach morals, and yet you must confess that the morals to not directly draw the inner life after themselves — indeed that true morals can only be found as a consequence of the inner life.

285. The parables of Christ have already been so exploited in the moral, ethical direction that it would be very difficult for me to say anything new in this respect, let alone something better than what has already been said a hundred times. — I will therefore limit myself primarily to the substantial, bodily, or material meaning, and indeed to emphasising this all the more dearly, as the moral rebirth without a preceding bodily rebirth is an impossibility (see § 66).

286. After these preceding comments we may finally be in a position to move on to positive Christianity and to portray both the inner life and the method for it clearly from the texts of the sacred scripture.

287. We begin this undertaking with the first two verses of the gospel of John:

> "In the beginning was the Word, and the Word was with God, and the Word was God. The same was in the beginning with God."

288. This text, so simple that a child can grasp it, has turned through our leisurely thought into the sphinx. Our theologians have become as one in understanding this "*word*" to be Christ. But why in this case did the apostle, in order to evade all difficulty, not rather express it thus:

> "In the beginning was Christ, and Christ was with God, and Christ was God."

The Christian Church has failed to give the answer to this question.

289. In contrast to the Church, the rationalists sought to identify the *word* with cognition, knowing, mind, so that they finally felt forced to make the claim:

> "God is the highest reason."

290. To thus imagine God as the highest reason is the greatest nonsense. Nonetheless this nonsense has infected the entire way of thinking of educated society. Hence such immense worth is placed on learnedness through the attendance

at schools and universities as if we would become through our cleverness more and more similar to God.

291. School instruction has its worth, but all sciences are of earthly nature, and have worth and significance only for the short span of life. For the other side they are completely unimportant. The inhabitant of the steppes in the most backward corner of a wasteland in which the refinements of life's needs, of civilisation never penetrated, and never will penetrate, can obtain the inner life just as well as the professor at his lectern, indeed the latter has no advantage over the former at all; both can only become blessed by the same method, both must swallow the language powers of nature, the *word*, into themselves until it becomes flesh and blood in them.

292. The nature of God is nothing but pure strength. God does not need contemplation, considering like a human when he wants to create something. Were that the case, then God would admittedly be the highest reason. But this entire idea of thinking of God as an infinitely clever human is, as I will show in a moment, absurd, unnatural. —

293. When humans think about something, that indeed means, as I have already mentioned earlier (§§ 215–236), nothing more than the endeavour of bringing the movements of God into the consciousness. What is though now foolish to think is that God must bring his movements into his consciousness to be able to move!!! — — —

294. God creates, i.e. he moves, and when he moves, this movement is a form, and this form has a character, a spirit, a sense, an understanding; and the simplest forms, the simplest characters, the simplest understandings are the letters, and for that reason God is called the word.

295. The nature of God is nothing but pure, absolute, perfect strength, so that each of his works carries the stamp of perfection in itself. God creates, and what he creates is wise, and what he creates is beautiful. The wisdom and beauty lie in and of themselves in the nature of an absolutely perfect power, for God is qualitatively indivisible.

296. If God had to think with the execution of his works in order to make them wise and beautiful, then he would not be qualitatively indivisible, there would thus have to be yet

something outside his nature whose help and support he required — but then God would not be God — instead that something would then be God. In whatever way we may think about it, to the concept of "God" there belongs an absolute freedom, and since this is not present in thinking, God does not need thinking, and if he does not need thinking, then his nature also cannot be called the highest reason, for rational according to our linguistic usage are all those things which we find in agreement with the laws of nature after careful thought.

297. Now did the original law, the eternal strength, the word also have to be thought first in order to be put in agreement with itself!!!

298. The limited human idea of God as the highest reason leads to such confusion.

299. God is nothing but pure strength, and his strength knows no enemy, and no obstacle, and no difficulty, and no contemplation, but instead only absolute freedom, hence God is nothing more than an absolutely free power, i.e. perfect, i.e. qualitatively indivisible and quantitatively immeasurable.

300. But the eternal strength rests in the word and the letters are the word. The spirit of the letters is nothing, however, but pure strength which reveals itself in wisdom and beauty. Anyone who does not feel and experience that is not human at all, they know neither themselves, nor God, nor the spirit of nature, they are yet a dead gravedigger, and there is no other advice in heaven or on earth than to think the letters into themselves for as long as until they sense their character, their power and strength, then they will have arisen from death into life and will rejoice over it to the eternal praise of God all the more as they now certainly know that it can never be taken from them anymore. Then Christ has arisen in them and they are blessed by the sweet names (power and nature) of our Lord and Saviour Jesus Christ.

301. When a human has once become conscious of the spirit of the letters and identified their ego with this spirit, then they have also obtained absolute freedom, as it then stands written:

My Father worketh hitherto, and I work. John 5:17.

The Father knows nothing more than to work and create, and the son, the human born again in Christ, the inner life, lives likewise as the complete image of God in full freedom.

302. The spirit of the Father, in and of itself, lives in eternal clairvoyance, clairaudience, and clairsentience. Humans must bring these powers to life in themselves through the letter practice, then they will not talk of themselves anymore, but rather what they will hear, they will speak, and what is in the future, they will presage. John 16:15.

303. Then the human becomes perfect, for it is not he who then creates and takes effect, but instead the Father, God, who resides in him, that is the one who does the works. John 14:10. (§§ 243–253.)

304. The apostle John now continues:

"All things were made by him; and without him was not any thing made that was made." John 1:3.

This is thus the key to all knowledge, to all absolute power, to all the miracles of creation.

305. How that is to be understood, I believe I have already mentioned ad nauseam (§ 135, § 146 ff., § 156, § 160 ff.), it is only necessary to expressly mention that even the inner life is not made without it. Therefore when a human wants to bring Christ from death into life in himself, when he wants to obtain the true inner life, then he must take up the language powers of nature, the word, creatively within himself and let the Son of Man form from it.

306. There is no other way, no other method, for there was no other *name* given to us within which we will become blessed than the *name* of our Lord Jesus Christ.

The *name* of our Lord Jesus Christ is, however, just the language powers of God become flesh and blood — for the name of God is his activity which makes itself known in the word and as the word, i.e. as letters.

307. Anyone who by the name Jesus Christ understands an arbitrary conceptual description and suggests that within it humanity must become blessed, they cheat themselves out of their inner life because they are transforming the nature and the power of God into the fixed idea of a vapid arbitrary thing. For if everything that is made was made only by the word, then by that it is expressed that if God wants to create some-

thing, then he must move himself. God is thus not a sorcerer who can conjure something without moving (§ 157); but instead his creating is his movement and his movement is his language, his *word*. From that you know clearly the boundaries of the omnipotence, and therefore the view of those who then suggest that God can by means of his omnipotence make 2 × 2 = 4 today and 5 tomorrow is an entirely crazy one which does not deserve a rebuttal.

308. "In him was life; and the life was the light of men. And the light shineth in darkness; and the darkness comprehended it not. [...] That was the true Light, which lighteth every man that cometh into the world." John 1:4, 5, 9.

309. In the word, in the language powers lies life, and these language powers are the light of humanity. These language powers penetrate the darkness of the earthly man of thought, but although the senses see, hear, feel, smell, taste these language powers, the spirit of these language powers, the true light, remain incomprehensible to them. But it is the true light which illuminates *all* humans who come into this world, for the language powers of nature are not withheld from anyone, whoever it might be, they are a common good, and anyone who always takes up these powers into themselves through wanting, thinking, and feeling (§ 208 ff.), they are escaping the bonds of darkness and sitting themselves as liberated son of the eternal strength at the right hand of the majesty of God.

310. It is not to be stated any simpler, any clearer than John expressed the fundamental laws of life in the first nine verses of his gospel. And it remains quite incomprehensible how these few words could be misunderstood so badly.

311. You should think it would have to enlighten anyone that a light which illuminates **all** humans can only be understood as not Christ in his *person*, but rather in his *universality*, i.e. only as the spirit of language become flesh and blood in Christ.

312. The objectively historical Christ illuminates even now only the smallest part of the human race, thus it cannot be the light which illuminates *all* humans.

313. Anyone who does not recognise that Christ is only a representative, a son of this light — whereas by contrast the true

light is everywhere, omnipresent, and furthermore wants and wishes nothing at all but to illuminate and awaken humans to the true life — they do not know the nature of Christ at all.

314. Woe, if all were lost who never heard of Christ. Such a thought is incompatible with the idea of an absolutely prefect being and does without any necessity, any consequence.

315. But those who want to see in reason this light which illuminates *all* humanity are no less in error.

316. Reason is related to the true light like the moonlight to the sun. Reason is not independent light, but rather only a weak reflection of it; for reason is a product which must first be developed in the human, which is ignited in the human, as soon as he just turns to, dedicates himself to the true light, to the language powers of nature. For these language powers penetrate through the natural channels of the five senses into the disposition of the human and awaken language. Through language, however, the human brings the impressions of the language powers of nature to consciousness, and the experience of these impressions is what we call reason. Consequently reason is only a strained, inactive state; for where there is no language, there no reason develops either, which can be seen in those who are deaf and dumb and for whom no language was taught by means of another sense through signs or whatever.

317. In the eleventh verse, John leaps away from the generality and passes to the person of Christ, while nonetheless symbolising it, i.e. using his person simply as the definition of the general original law:

"He came unto his own, and his own received him not. But as many as received him, to them gave he power to become the sons of God, even to them that believe on his name: Which were born, not of blood, nor of the will of the flesh, nor of the will of man, but of God. And the Word was made flesh, and dwelt among us, (and we beheld his glory, the glory as of the only begotten of the Father,) full of grace and truth."[*]

318. The Church considered these words to be a proof that Christ is the word in its absolute significance, i.e. is identical with God, not only qualitatively, but also quantitatively. This

---

[*] [Tr.: John 1:11–14.]

assumption is not justified in the least by the preceding verses.

319. Anyone who believes in the name of Christ, i.e. in the inner life, i.e. anyone who believes in the possibility of being able to take up creatively in themselves the word, i.e. the language powers of the universal, and of forming from it a new spiritual body, to them Christ gives the word, the power of becoming a child of God. Thus not only Christ is a child of God, but anyone who awakens the inner life in themselves. The historical Christ had no other advantage over any other human at all than that he had no physical father. As perfect definition of the inner life, it must not and could not be otherwise. The prophets recognised that perfect true redemption and salvation of the human race which had degenerated into sensuality and worldly desire was only then to be hoped for and expected when, in the midst of the civilisation contaminated by vices and horrors of all sorts, an original son, a primitive man were to arise again, vanquishing all temptations of a refined depravity, to realise through his life and works the original law in itself and radiate as perfect ideal to all languages, peoples, races, and times for emulation in inviolable majesty for ever and ever.

320. Probably even despite this depravity every other human could seek the inner life — only the depravity, which infects the organs of each one through the carnal creation, because indeed in the man's seed all the characteristics of the individual, both good and evil, are contained germinally (embryonically) — (the original sin, as it is called) would never have tolerated such a high perfection, and without this high — infallible — immaculate divine perfection all of humanity would have sunk down with the already habitual general depravity as far as that bestiality in which all the wild peoples find themselves today.

321. Indeed it is not believed that the wild peoples are in the original state, in the state of childhood — the primary period of their age. No, humans went forth from the hand of God perfect, and bear the living word of God as infallibly within themselves as the animals bear their instincts. — All the wild peoples found themselves at once in the state of development and civilisation and sank down through vice and horror until

finally the last knowledge of their divine origin was extinguished and deepest night and barbarism nipped all the noble and beautiful in the bud.

322. Had Christ not appeared, then all the peoples of earth would have finally sunk into this disconsolate wildness, and if this horrible state had become common over the entire inhabited earth, then the divine judgement would have struck infallibly. Through evil, inward wrath, through the horror of humanity, the earth would have shattered, the fire seething in it would have split water into its components and set fire to the entire atmosphere. Thus the globe would have dissolved into atoms and been transformed into a new chaos. (2 Peter 3:7–10.)

323. Christ saved humanity from this fate, that is why he is the king of kings, the lord of Christianity before whom all knees must bend.

324. Had Christ not offered resistance to the temptations, had he thus not given the lie to the word of the prophets, had he, instead of giving his life for the truth, freed himself from the persecution of the Pharisees, then he would have indeed been able to lead a quite leisurely life, but humanity would have hurried inexorably towards its downfall.

325. The prophets recognised this consequence. To them the future of the human race was vivid before their eyes. They recognised in spirit that only a primitive man could bring salvation for the fallen human race. As soon as they recognised this necessity of the prophetic spirit, they foretold the appearance of Christ, and consequently the divination of the prophets as the word of God is the father of Christ.

326. The word of the earthly human dies away in the air, it is like the smoke which climbs into the air and then vanishes.

327. But the word of the spirit which the reborn human (the inner, true life) expresses is a power which knows no obstacle, no resistance, is a power with does not rest and does not take a break until fulfillment approaches.

328. The German prophet Schiller recognised this connection when he said:

> "Genius [the inner life] and nature stand in eternal alliance.

Part 3: The Evidence of Sacred Scripture

What the one promises, the other certainly achieves."*

329. And Christ expressed the same law of nature with the words:
"Whatsoever ye shall ask the Father in my name, he will give it you." John 16:23.
"Heaven and earth shall pass away: but my words shall not pass away." Mark 13:31.
"And all things, whatsoever ye shall ask in prayer, *believing* [i.e. so you feel the spirit of the prayer as feeling of life = inner life], ye shall receive." Matthew 21:22.

330. The word of the prophets, as word of God, sought and worked for so long until it found in the Virgin Mary receptivity for absorption. Then it poured itself into her body and produced Jesus of Nazareth.

331. Jesus Christ was then born, a primitive man, a new Adam stood in the midst of an indeed developed, but depraved civilisation. He perceived the word of God within himself, recognised the laws of life, felt the necessity of identifying his *ego* with the word of God, i.e. with the language powers of the universe, through development of the inner spiritual body. This goal he followed inexorably, vanquished all temptations, vanquished sensuality, ambition, the charms and enticements of the world and finally death. He recognised that he was now one with God, his father, that the word in him became of a different nature, of a spiritual flesh and blood, and then he pronounced himself as the definition of the true inner life, as the highest good, as absolute perfection, as the qualitative identity of God!!!

332. With this interpretation, we again come into conflict with the Church because it suggests Christ had been already eo ipso† God, right at birth, indeed from eternity. (§§ 117–119.)

333. Christ was as word, as inner life from eternity qualitatively one with God; but the historical Jesus of Nazareth indeed heard the word of God already as a child pure and unbroken within himself, even because his organs were not altered by the original sin, only, to the extent he did not obey

---
* [Tr.: from Friedrich von Schiller's poem Kolumbus (1795).]
† [Tr.: eo ipso = by that very act.]

this word of God, also to the extent *he* had tasted instead of just the fruits of the tree of life, i.e. enjoying the language powers of the universe, also tasted of the fruits of the tree of knowledge of good and evil, i.e. also to the extent Christ considered himself to be identical with his spirit and had believed he could by means of this identity want *himself*, know *himself*, live and change according to his *own* arbitrariness, then to that extent the word of God would not have become flesh and blood in him and even *he* would have fallen prey to the fate of the rest of humanity.

334. Christ was therefore not already in and of himself the word, but rather he first won himself the identity with it; for it is indeed said expressly: the word **became** flesh. It does not stand written: the word was flesh from eternity, but rather it became flesh. But this event is not to be understood as the birth of Christ, but rather as the inner life which Christ awoke in himself. Through the birth of Christ the word did not yet become flesh, but instead it was only like in other humans in the body which it animated. The word first became flesh and blood in Christ when Christ, taught by the voice of the spirit, thought, breathed, swallowed into himself the language powers of nature, the letters, for so long as until they became flesh and blood in him, until they penetrated his entire body, until it was nothing but pure word.

335. The first 14 verses of the gospel of John contain the doctrine of the Christian religion in its absolute generality and simplicity, and are of such importance that I feel forced to establish a few parallels for clarification.

336. Thus as John began the doctrine of the laws of life with the words: In the beginning was the Word, and the Word was with God, and the Word was God, so a musician could as introduction to the basso continuo say:

　In the beginning there were the 7 tones.
　And the 7 tones were with music.
　And the music was the 7 tones.

337. In the old so-called heathen times when you personified all characteristics, powers, arts, and sciences, and erected temples and altars to these powers considered as persons, a priest of Apollo could have said:

　In the beginning there was the music.

And the music was Apollo.

And Apollo was the music.

338. Thus as the music consists of the seven tones, the word consists of the letters, and just as the musician must make music with the seven tones up and down for as long as until the musical ear achieves absolute infallibility, so must humans think the alphabet into themselves for as long as until the spirit of the letters lives and weaves as absolute, pure, unbroken word of God in them.

339. In order to continue the parallels, you could now say:

2.* The music was in the beginning with Apollo.

3. All things (which sound) were made by it; and without it was not anything (sounding) made that was made.

4. In it was the scale; and the scale was the light (the harmony) of all musicians.

5. And the light shineth in darkness; and the unmusical ear comprehended it not.

9. That was the true Light (the true harmony), which lighteth every musician that cometh into the world.

340. Now if the history of music had demonstrated a period where true harmony had almost completely died out, and where then suddenly a musical genius, like Mozart, had arisen, and indeed been unrecognised by his contemporaries, indeed persecuted and mocked, although pronouncing the pure doctrine of harmony again, you could continue in the parallels:

11. Mozart came unto his own, and his own received him not.

12. But as many as received him, to them gave he power to become the sons of Apollo, even to them that believe on his name:

13. Which were born, not of blood, nor of the will of the flesh, nor of the will of man, but of Apollo.

14. And the Music was made flesh, and dwelt among us, (and we beheld his (Mozart's) glory, the glory as (if it were) of the only begotten of Apollo,) full of melody and harmony.

---

*   [Tr.: i.e. parallel with verse 2 of the gospel of John.]

341. A similar parallel under similar assumptions could be made with painting, as follows:

1. In the beginning was the light, and the light was with the sun, and the sun was the light.

2. The same was in the beginning with the sun.

3. All coloured things were made by it; and without it was no colour made that was made.

4. In it was the beauty; and the beauty was the law of painting.

5. And the law of painting shineth in darkness; and the tasteless comprehended it not.

9. That was the true beauty, which delighteth every painter that cometh into the world.

10. The beauty was in the world, and the world was made by it, and the world knew it not.

11. Raphael came unto his own, and his own received him not.

12. But as many as received him, to them gave he power to become the sons of beauty, even to them that believe on his name (school):

14. And painting was made flesh, and dwelt among us, (and we beheld (in Raphael) its glory, the glory as of the only begotten of the ideal beauty,) full of lustre and symmetry.

342. Such parallels you could establish in any field, but I leave this to the readers themselves, hoping that they do not go astray when a lower sphere will not deliver a perfect parallel to the brilliant prologue of John.

343. Christ is qualitatively one with God, but not quantitatively, and he obtained this qualitative union through the letter practice, and the discipleship of Christ consists in that we, like him, think the letters into ourselves for so long as until their spirit develops the true inner life in us.

344. "Jesus saith unto them, *My meat is* to do the will of him that sent me, and to finish his work." John 4:34. — The moral interpretation here is simple, the intrinsic interpretation, however, is the letter thinking. For when Christ took the will of God as meat for himself, nothing else can be understood by the will of God than the thought letters, to the extent God wants and can want nothing else than himself. He himself is,

however, nothing else but word. But if someone wants to take this word for themselves, then they must just devote themselves to the language powers of nature and take up into themselves the elements of thinking, the letters.

345. And Christ said furthermore: "Verily I say unto you, Except ye be converted, and become as little children, ye shall not enter into the kingdom of heaven." Matthew 18:3. — The moral interpretation here is that we should be harmless like children; the intrinsic interpretation, however, is that we must learn our A B C like the children again. — Hey, that is a hard imposition! What scholar may you surely ask to climb down from the proud steed of his bold ideas, to deny the fruits of his weak knowledge, and simply think the letters into himself like a child!!! And indeed this activity is the simpler, the better, for with our cleverness we chase away the spirit of the letters, but in the simplicity lies the true receptivity. The woman must be receptive, however, for impregnation, otherwise all the wealth of creation runs empty.

346. Christ also spoke about it: I thank thee, O Father, Lord of heaven and earth, because thou hast hid these things from the wise and prudent, and hast revealed them unto babes.*

347. And Christ said again: "If I wash thee not, thou hast no part with me. Simon Peter saith unto him, Lord, not my feet only, but also my hands and my head. Jesus saith to him, He that is washed needeth not save to wash his feet, but is clean every whit". John 13:8–10. In these words the moral interpretation of washing the feet, namely humility, is not expressed, but instead merely the intrinsic interpretation which wants to say as much as that humans must learn to feel the spirit of the letters firstly thinking in the feet, and that, if only the feet are first animated spiritually, are raised to the true life, the rest of the body will follow of itself.

348. Here Christianity stands in stark contrast to the principle of our schools. In the latter humans have nothing more than a head. The brain is crammed full for so long until it finally loses all agreement with the rest of the body and considers all the other organs to be lumps of flesh and muscle which stand far below it and only in the service of physical

---

*   [Tr.: Matthew 11:25.]

animality. Even the education of the head, however, is not a living one, but rather just mechanical. They do not teach the head perhaps to think, to preserve God, but instead it is merely a container into which as many ideas as possible are mechanically pumped. Thus the head becomes nothing more than an intellectual rumination machine and the rest of the body is dead, spiritless, ossified!!! — — —

349. The true inner life by contrast follows the same series of steps as the outer life. Just as the child must first learn to run, walk, and stand, the spiritual human must first experience their ego in the feet, and they can only achieve that by learning to think letters in their feet.

350. Once the feet are first animated spiritually, the entire body will animate itself gradually by itself.

351. That is the baptism of fire which does not go downward like the water baptism of John, but instead upwards and penetrates flesh and bone and the marrow in the bones. As it then stands written: For the word of God is quick, and powerful, and sharper than any two-edged sword, piercing even to the dividing asunder of soul and spirit, and of the joints and marrow, and is a discerner of the thoughts and intents of the heart. (Hebrews 4:12.)

352. And John said: I indeed baptize you with water unto repentance. But he that cometh after me is mightier than I, whose shoes I am not worthy to bear: he shall baptize you with the Holy Ghost, and with fire. Matthew 3:11.

353. Christ himself also had to undergo this baptism of fire, and hence Christ said: I am come to send fire on the earth; and what will I, if it be already kindled? But I have a baptism to be baptized with; and how am I straitened till it be accomplished! Luke 12:49–50. This baptism of fire is depicted symbolically by the suffering and dying, but everyone must undergo these pains who awakes the inner life in themselves because the spirit of the letters once alive is a burning fire which consumes all that is impure, earthly, and sinful!

354. If someone taken with emotion senses a cold trickle down the back, their hair bristles, and they feel strangely blown over, they should just think that John has baptised them. But after John comes Christ, the inner life, who bap-

tises with fire which begins in the feet and is not cold, but rather burns and consumes all that is impure, sinful, earthly.

355. Now as soon as the organs of the human are animated spiritually by the letter practice, new tongues occur all-over in all parts of the body, i.e. the entire body which was previously dead begins to speak as it stands written: For he that speaketh in an unknown tongue speaketh not unto men, but unto God: for no man understandeth him; howbeit in the spirit he speaketh mysteries. 1 Corinthians 14:2. — For if I pray in an unknown tongue, my spirit prayeth, but my understanding is unfruitful. 1 Corinthians 14:14.

356. These new tongues are nothing more than the spiritual activity of all the organs of which we become conscious, for the spirit in humans is in all limbs, organs, flesh and blood, innards and bones. But just as a church organ sounds differently through every register, so too is the activity of the spirit in each organ a different one.

357. This speaking in tongues works infectiously as soon as someone enters an assembly of the spiritually animated or the reborn, as then stands written: And they of the circumcision which *believed* were astonished, as many as came with Peter, because that on the Gentiles also was poured out the gift of the Holy Ghost. For they heard them speak with *tongues*, and magnify God. Apostles 10:45–46.

358. As long as there were still the reborn, for as long did the gift of the holy spirit pour itself over everyone. But when heathenry migrated en masse to Christianity, the letter practice was forgotten, the inner life vanished, the gifts of the holy spirit fell silent, and now the Church has only the skeleton of Christianity, but the spirit has fled.

359. This contagion of new tongues rests on the vibrations of the word which once in action sets in harmony everything about it, and this contagion has many analogies in visible nature. Two pendulum clocks, for example, which rest on the same, firm foundation, receive in the course of time the same swing. —

360. Paul speaks most clearly about the bodily rebirth or about the inner life in his first letter to the Corinthians, 15:13–58.

13. "But if there be no resurrection of the dead, then is Christ not risen".

361. Here Paul places the divine nature of Christ on the same level with all other humans. This verse 13 says quite clearly that Christ is not resurrected from the dead because he perhaps possessed as divinity the omnipotence for it — but rather because it lies in the nature of the human to produce a new spiritual body, and this spiritual body brings immortality with it.

362. Reading further:

22. For as in Adam (outer life) all die, even so in Christ (inner life) shall all be made alive.

40. There are also celestial *bodies*, and bodies terrestrial: but the glory of the celestial is one, and the glory of the terrestrial is another.

44. It is sown a natural body; it is raised a spiritual body.

46. Howbeit that was not first which is spiritual (inner life), but that which is natural; and afterward that which is spiritual.

363. Therefore when the bodily and moral rebirth is achieved, the true inner life is the way, the truth, and the life (John 14:6), is our righteousness which makes us pure from all our sins (1 John 1:7), likewise the spirit of Christ which was before Abraham was (John 8:58), in a word: *Christ in us*.

364. The inner life is the way because without inner life nobody can get to know God (Luke 10:22); it is the truth because only the inner life can hear the voice of the spirit unbroken, likewise the absolute truth; and finally the life, for the earthly life is only an apparent life. The inner life in its maturity is beyond sickness and death, and alone deserves therefore the name life. The earthly existence is compared to the inner life just a vegetative process, and the former relates to the latter like lead and iron to gold and platinum, like a house of clay and half-timber to a house of ivory, like must to alcohol, etc.

365. The inner life is our true righteousness; for the human of external senses and the world is always a selfish animal. The bestiality of the outer human reveals itself in all circumstances if it is not held back by fear or through convenience, or through the superiority of the inner life. Fear and conveni-

ence are not righteousness because they have their main focus not in, but rather outside themselves. The inner life, however, is based as the living word of God on itself, it is therefore the true righteousness, it is a matter of simple arithmetic on which you can be tested.

366. The inner life is finally Christ within us, who was before there was Abraham, for Christ was already in paradise. He is the true image of God which had faded in Adam. The inner life is the promised snake crusher who stamps on the head of the snake, of selfishness, and is bitten by it in the verse*.

367. Christ is the representative of the true inner life. Anyone who believes in him (John 11:25) and *follows* him (John 8:12) will live even if he dies straightaway, he will truly live even if he straightaway dies in his selfishness and in his earthly body.

368. Without Christ we cannot do anything. (John 15:5.) Without inner life we cannot do any works of the spirit.

369. Christ and the Father are one (John 10:30), the inner life and the divinity are one like the sunbeam and the sun are also one, but the Father is greater than I (John 14:28).

370. Christ claims to be God's son, nowhere for himself alone, but rather only for the inner life, and anyone who possesses the inner life in the same perfection also stands on the same level with him, for its stands written: I said, *Ye* are gods? If he called them gods, unto whom the word of God came, and the scripture cannot be broken; Say ye of him, whom the Father hath sanctified, and sent into the world, Thou blasphemest; because I said, I am the Son of God? John 10:34–36.

371. It furthermore stands written: Be ye therefore perfect, even as *your* Father which is in heaven is perfect. (Matthew 5:48.)

372. It is enough for the disciple that he be as his master. (Matthew 10:25.)

373. For whosoever shall do the will of my Father which is in heaven, the same is my brother, and sister, and mother. (Matthew 12:50.)

374. I ascend unto *my* Father, and *your* Father; and to *my* God, and *your* God. (John 20:17.)

---

*   [Tr.: cf. Luke 10:19, John 3:14–15, Psalms 91:13, and Genesis 3:15.]

375. That they all may be one; as thou, Father, art in me, and I in thee, that *they* also may be one in us. (John 17:21.)

376. And the glory which thou gavest me I have given them; that they may be one, *even as we are one*. John 17:22.

377. For whom he did foreknow (i.e. those who awaken the inner life in themselves), he also did predestinate *to be conformed to the image of his Son*, that he might be the firstborn among many brethren. Romans 8:29.

378. To him that overcometh will I grant to sit with me in my throne, even as I also overcame, and am set down with my Father in his throne. Revelations 3:21.

379. Verily I say unto you, That he shall make him ruler over *all* his goods. Matthew 24:47 etc.

380. In so far as the lad who gives the servants food at the right time — i.e. to the extent the human nourishes his spiritual characteristics during the duration of his earthly life through the language powers of nature and thereby produces his inner life — is placed above *all* goods, i.e. is placed above *all* powers and capabilities which are contained in the nature of the spirit, in the being of God, he is indeed qualitatively one with God and therefore stands also with Christ on the same level, and Christ has no advantage over all the others who have awoken the inner life in themselves like him than that by his life and works he lights up as a living example, shows the aim of his life again, and gives the means which can lead there. As a result he has indeed eternal claim to our thankfulness and veneration, but he is not a being of a higher sort, even less the universal divinity which can never quantitatively individualise in one body.

381. Christ, the inner life, is the renewed image of God. For it is then that the human is born anew, from (a material) of water and spirit, thus he cannot see the kingdom of God. (John 3:5. 1 Peter 1:23.)

382. **The kingdom of God cometh not with observation: Neither shall they say, Lo here! or, lo there! for, behold, the kingdom of God is within you.** (Luke 17:20–21.)

383. How despite these texts you can only attribute worth and significance to the historically objective Christ, but can almost

ignore the subjective Christ in us as inessential, that is inexplicable to me.

384. The common man is not spatially separated from the kingdom of God, but rather only specifically separated. For anyone who ever awakens their inner life through the letter practice, in them free spiritual powers begin their activity and these powers are one matter in us, and wherever they obtain consciousness in the human, there the kingdom of God becomes visible.

385. Since we now pray: Our Father, who art in heaven, and the heaven is in us, so too thus is the Father, the Son, and the Holy Spirit in us, i.e. in the inner life.

386. For the human of the external senses, the doctrine of the inner life is nonsense (1 Corinthians 2:14), but blessed are those who do not yet see the inner life and yet believe in it. (John 20:29.)

387. The inner life is the mustard seed, "Which indeed is (in its beginning: in dream life) the least of all seeds: but when it is grown, it is the greatest among herbs, and becometh a tree, so that the birds of the air (the desires of humanity) come and lodge in the branches thereof". (Matthew 13:32.)

388. Without inner life the desires and wishes of humans know no rest and repose. When someone is rich, they want to become even richer. When they have power, they want to become even more powerful. For the sensory human, his wishes are a scourge which chases and drives and fatigues him without interruption, without stopping, without standstill, until he finally sinks exhausted into the arms of death. — And what is the fruit of his efforts?! What is the reward for his deeds?! Dust, transience, death.

389. Foolish human race! When will you grow tired of serving as dogsbody in the building of the tower of Babel!

390. May the attraction of creation be yet so great, may the beauties which nature offers us, for eye and ear, for the palate and for the nose, be yet so charming, may the most beautiful ideas which anyone has ever expressed sound yet so sublime, yet so blissful, yet so spiritual — the *power* which brings forth *everything* must be more beautiful than everything made, than everything that has become.

391. Nature can pass away, the world can plunge again into a chaos — but the *power*, the eternal strength of the universe can never perish.

392. Leave off though, foolish human race, from hanging your heart on the *creations* of the power. Hang your entire heart, all your wishes, wanting and yearning on the *power itself*, seek it incessantly in the word and do not let up until the spirit of all the powers, the letters, becomes your inalienable property — then your desire will be rested, for in the power itself is more contentment than a human can grasp, wish, want, and understand.

393. The actual idolatry consists in that the human shows reverence not to the creator, but instead to the created, not to the power, but instead to the effects. — God wants to wed himself to humanity and produce in them a new sacred being. — But now if the human weds himself not with God, the power, the word, the letters — but instead with something that has become, with one-sided ideas, with earthly wishes, plans, hobbies, i.e. exercises them in himself, accommodates them in himself for so long as until the desire for money, positions of honour, rank, title, etc. has become flesh and blood in him — then he is a heathen, an idolator, and practises fornication in the sense of the scripture, which according to the 17th and 18th chapters of Revelations is a horror before God.

394. The inner life is the leaven which a woman (who shall bear the son of man) took, and hid in *three* measures of meal (with skin, flesh, and bones) until the entire body from the tips of the toes to the top of one's head is nothing but pure word. (Matthew 13:33.)

395. The inner life is the son of man like the butterfly is the son of the caterpillar, for the inner life is the fruit of the outer human, produced by the spirit of God.

396. It is usually thought that when Christ called himself son of man, he wanted by that to signify his humanity. That is not so. Christ wanted by that only to bestow the most correct title on himself so that the true understanding of his person and his mission becomes all the easier. For it stands written:

397. And no man hath ascended up to heaven, but he that came down from heaven, even the *Son of man* which is in heaven. (John 3:13.) But his humanity now did not come

Part 3: The Evidence of Sacred Scripture

from heaven and was also not in heaven — but the inner life is from heaven, for the inner life is in us.

398. It furthermore stands written: Except ye eat the flesh of the Son of man, and drink his blood, ye have no life in you. (John 6:53–56.)
If the son of man signifies the humanity of Christ, then this text would, like the previous one, be inexplicable. The flesh and blood of the *son of* man, i.e. of the inner life, is the word, and this we must eat and drink, i.e. the language powers of the letters must also become a spiritual flesh and blood in us, must form a new solid connection, a new body, the inner life in us.

399. It furthermore stands written that the Father "hath given him authority to execute judgment also, *because he is the Son of man*."* Here again the son of man cannot describe the humanity of Christ, as for the humanity of Christ it would be entirely impossible to hold judgement over all humanity. To the contrary, that which every human produces in themselves is their natural judge. That which the human produces through their vanity, vices, moods, wishes — or through their beliefs and their virtues, that is their son of man which will one day hold judgement over them.

400. The inner life is furthermore the five wise virgins (Matthew 25:1–13), the five spiritual senses which also then still see, hear, smell, taste, feel, when the five foolish virgins, the five earthly senses sink down and are extinguished because they lack oil.

401. The inner life is the precious hidden treasure in the field of our body (Matthew 13:44), for the sake of which a human goes and sells all his earthly wishes, plans, tendencies, hobbies, and hobby horses in order to dedicate his heart solely to this treasure.

402. The inner life is the seed which a farmer throws on the land. (Mark 4:26.) "For the earth bringeth forth fruit of herself; first the blade, then the ear, after that the full corn in the ear." (Mark 4:28.) When humans take up the language powers, the letters, within themselves, the human body brings from itself first of all the dream life, after that the inner

---
* [Tr.: John 5:27.]

life, after that the son of man. But when the fruit is brought, then the harvest is there.

403. Anyone who finds their earthly life in sensuous pleasures, in earthly endeavours will lose the inner life. But anyone who loses their earthly life for *my* sake will find the inner life. (Matthew 10:39.)

404. Anyone who has the inner life is given so that he has plenty. (Luke 12:44.) But anyone who does not have the inner life, from them the outer life which he meant to have will also be taken. (Matthew 13:12.)

405. Where two (the inner and outer life) become one (Matthew 18:19), why is it that they want to beg that it shall come again to them from my Father in heaven. (John 14 & 15:7–14.) That these two are not two outer humans can be ascertained very easily by the test.

406. At the future coming of the son of man, two shall be in the field, the inner life will be taken, the external will be left. Two shall grind at a mill, the inner life will be taken and the external will be left. (Matthew 24:40–41.)

407. Let the dead bury their dead. (Matthew 8:22.) Let those who are dead in the inner life bury the corpses of the dead.

408. And no man knoweth the Son, but the Father. (Matthew 11:27.) And nobody knows the powers of the inner life, save only the spirit; and nobody knows the spirit, save only the inner life and those to whom it will reveal the same.

409. For my yoke is easy, and my burden is light. (Matthew 11:30), the yoke of the inner life is easy and its burden is light. For a thing which exists by itself is no burden anymore. But that which must constantly be worried for its existence (status quo), that is a burden. E.g. bare iron rusts in the air and rust is not iron anymore; that is why you have eternal trouble with it. But platinum does not and cannot rust, compared with iron, that is to say: my yoke is easy. The outer life consists of thousands of needs all of whose satisfaction lies outside of ones absolute power and is connected with lesser or greater difficulty. If these needs now could not be satisfied anymore, or the relationships alter themselves and with them the satisfaction of those endeavours to which you dedicate your entire life are thwarted, then ill humour, worries, sorrow, unease, wailing, illness, misery, and finally death comes.

Hence the external is only **one** burden from morning until evening and the common human also has no higher aim than to rid themselves of this burden or at least make it impalpable through bustle, enjoyments, and distractions of all sorts. He is like a bankrupt who does not like to make his true state known only to awaken in the end all the more terribly. There is only *one* true method of escaping the burden of the outer life and that is the inner life, the son of man, Christ within us.

410. Christ is David's lord and son (Matthew 22:45), the inner life is David's lord and son. For the lord and son are the same thing here. The inner life is the son of man, and this son is the lord who shall reign over the outer life. For if the outer life has also fulfilled all the laws and instructions, then it must nevertheless say: We are unprofitable servants: we have done that which was our duty to do (for our master, the inner life). (Luke 17:10.)

411. The inner life, the rebirth, the son of man, the paradise, the wisdom, the kingdom of God, the kingdom of heaven, the subjective Christ, Christ within us, the new Jerusalem, etc. are expressions which all express one and the same secret.

412. *Christ* taught this secret to his disciples clearly and comprehensibly — to the people by contrast only in parables, hence Christ spoke to his disciples: To you it is given to hear the secret of the kingdom of God, but to them out there (the people) it all comes through parables. (Mark 4:11.) Was this secret which Christ shared with his disciples in clear words — but to the people only in parables — was it perhaps the ten commandments? Those the people indeed knew; or was it the communion? That Jesus indeed only appointed later.

413. This secret of the kingdom of God was none other than that humans must take up the language powers of God within themselves and must have their inner life formed by it — i.e. Christ taught his disciples the letter practice whereby Christ himself had obtained the true life and had sat himself to the right of the majesty of God.

414. He taught the people this secret only in parables and justified this keeping of the secret by the words: "neither cast ye your pearls before swine". (Matthew 7:6.)

415. Christ did not like to teach the doctrine of the word publicly to the public at large, to every common man who rolled

like a pig in the muck and dreck of earthly greed, but instead limited himself to letting his disciples, i.e. those who possessed the receptivity for it, in on the doctrine of the living word of God. Even the disciples propagated this doctrine only orally and thus it could only happen that (when heathenry, when the heathenry sunken in sensuality, gluttony, opulence, horror, and lunacy passed in great numbers into Christianity) — the letter practice was entirely forgotten, although it is to be read everywhere between the lines in all the words and deeds of Christ.

416. This letter practice was not some invention of Christ, but rather it is the content of the most ancient rituals and mysteries of all religions, races, and languages.

417. Christ said: Think not that I am come to destroy the law, or the prophets: I am not come to destroy, but to fulfil. (Matthew 5:17.)

418. He also did not come to abolish the necessity of the letter practice — but instead to fulfill this activity, and thereby to show how far it brings humans, and what high perfection they can achieve, if they put the appropriate method to use diligently and assiduously.

419. That this original law, this letter practice, this original religion was already known in the most ancient times follows from the words: "And to Seth, to him also there was born a son; and he called his name Enos: then began men to call upon the name of the Lord." Genesis 4:26.

420. What then is the name of the Lord? Perhaps God, perhaps Jehovah? Perhaps Jupiter, perhaps Zeus, perhaps Brahma, perhaps Allfather?!!! — The name of the Lord is the language power of God, is the activity of God moving in the letters, is the word, is the inner life (see § 306).

421. When the human race was 235 years old, it had already distanced itself so far from the inner life and conceded to the outer life so much dominance already that it was considered good to make humans attentive to the necessity of not withdrawing from the language powers of nature because otherwise the true inner life would have to atrophy, i.e. you began to preach the Lord's name. Previously it was thus not necessary. The human recognised and felt this necessity by itself the way the migratory birds also know by themselves when

the winter comes and what they must do beforehand. — In the year 235, however, the flippancy was already so great that they ignored this necessity, and hence attention began to be drawn to it.

422. The entire Jewish history revolves about nothing more at all than about this letter practice, and the doctrine survived because of this amongst all the nations the longest with the Jews. With no other nation do we see all the morals, laws, customs, all the state institutions in such intimate connection with the doctrine of the word of God than with the Jews. Only that after the Flood this doctrine was never promulgated publicly anymore. The people were given the ten commandments and a moral way of life was desired of them. Where you found receptivity, there you gave in the schools of prophets special instruction in the doctrine of the living word of God, and Judea owed to this instruction its wisemen and prophets.

423. At the time of Christ, this simple letter practice was totally supplanted by a flaunting ceremonial service. Hence Christ also spoke reproachfully to the priests: Woe unto you, lawyers! for ye have taken away the *key of knowledge*: ye entered not in yourselves, and them that were entering in ye hindered. Luke 11:52. The priests and Levites found themselves flattered by the veneration of the people and gratified by the countless sacrifices. They thought that by virtue of their physical descent from Abraham they could not be lacking at all, and so the inner life became ever more foreign to them until in the end they did not comprehend at all anymore that the ancient promise —

"And the angel of the Lord called unto Abraham out of heaven the second time, And said, By myself have I sworn, saith the Lord, for because thou hast done this thing, and hast not withheld thy son, thine only son: That in blessing I will bless thee, and in multiplying I will multiply *thy seed* as the stars of the heaven, and as the sand which is upon the sea shore; and thy seed shall possess the gate of his enemies; And in *thy seed* shall all the nations of the earth be blessed; because thou hast obeyed my voice." Genesis 22:15–18.

— that ancient promise referred not to the *outer*, but rather to the *inner life*.

424. The book of Genesis and the story of Christ's suffering and, in the most magnificent measure, the Revelations of John are nothing but symbols of the inner life, where one follows the other, all objects treating the outer and inner life, where each symbol again and again has the two-fold significance, a bodily intrinsic one and an ethical moral one, both pronouncing for our benefit, for our teaching and instruction, the steps and the struggles, the development and deformities, the means and ways to the true inner life.

425. Thus this ancient promise will then be understood thus: The angel of the Lord called to Abraham from heaven. — Since heaven is inside the human, this angel was only the thought personified voice of the inner life. Thus the inner life spoke to Abraham:

> "because thou hast done this thing, and hast not withheld thy son, thine only son".

Our only son, the son of the outer human, is namely our outer business or artistic activity. The human must not idolise this and be smitten with themselves, but instead he must regard his works as being nothing next to the living word of God — i.e. the human must not regard all that which he creates and produces by means of his spiritual powers to be higher than the cause of these phenomena, than the spirit itself which as a part of God is alone entitled to the dignity of divinity.

426. Now because Abraham did that, God wants to bless his seed. This seed is again the inner life. This inner life shall yet become as numerous as the stars in the heavens; the inner life shall possess the gates of its enemies, the inner life shall thrash the heathens, all those who do not possess the inner life, with the iron rod, and in the inner life all the peoples of earth will be blessed, i.e. among all the peoples of the earth, whosoever awakens the inner life in themselves shall be blessed. And consequently then only those who do the works of Abraham, namely awaken the inner life in themselves, are the children of Abraham.

427. It is with the Christians these days similar to how it was with the Jews. *We* also think we will not lack at all because we are baptised in the name of Christ. Thus *we* too render homage to a dead outer ceremony, consider the observance of

this ceremony to be meritorious and stand as far as ever from the inner life, the living word, the eternal Christ.

428. The doctrine of the name of the Lord would once more have perished if the enormous ideal had not existed which Jesus established through his life and works, through his suffering and dying. The doctrine of the name of the Lord thereby obtained a living commentary for all times and races. Every doctrine can be twisted and made ridiculous — the life of Jesus is inviolable. This life is an eternal admonisher and caller, it is the worm that never dies and the fire which never goes out — which seethes and seethes on and on for so long as until humanity again takes up the path to truth.

429. But now it is time that the living word of God again became common amongst humanity. Now after eighteen centuries where the enormous ideal of Christ has reduced the horrors of the dark Middle Ages to the meekness and virtues of tame household animals — now humans must again seek and awaken the living word of God in themselves.

430. Germany, wake up and recognise your calling. You among all peoples on the entire earth must lead the way.

431. Come, you Germans, who still possess your receptivity of disposition to feel and take up in yourself the language powers of God — who are still pious enough, like Abraham, to not spare your own children — who can decide to become children and learn the A B C of the true inner life — come, you Germans, and awake through the letters the living word of God in yourselves, and hear what Christ says:

> "Verily I say unto you, All sins shall be forgiven unto the sons of men, and blasphemies wherewith soever they shall blaspheme". Mark 3:28. "And whosoever shall speak a word against the Son of man, it shall be forgiven him: but unto him that blasphemeth against the Holy Ghost it shall not be forgiven." Luke 12:10. Matthew 12:32.

432. Anyone who thus commits an outrage against God and e.g. swears in his suffering at the highest being (because the human would not indeed have desired his existence) — that can be forgiven, if he turns around and begs God for forgiveness.

433. Anyone who sins against the commandments of God can obtain forgiveness as soon as he makes good his wrong again.

If thus a slaveowner has a slave whipped to death, he can obtain forgiveness to the extent he seeks out the slave one day in eternity and persists with begging and imploring for so long as until his former slave forgives him, presses him to his heart, and they acknowledge and love each other as children of one and the same father.

434. Even the sins against the son of man can be forgiven. All who persecuted, crucified, mocked Christ can obtain forgiveness. All non-Christians who revile and persecute the person of Christ can obtain forgiveness. Indeed even those who sin against their own son of man, against the subjective Christ, like e.g. the prophet John, can again obtain rest and peace as soon as they see, confess, and again make right their wrong.

435. But whoever blasphemies the *holy spirit*, they will *never* be forgiven, neither in this, nor in that world.

God works and creates incessantly by his movements. And this activity is his language, his name, his almighty word. And these movements of the power of God have a character, a spirit, and this spirit streams from all movements and pours itself creatively into the disposition of humans as a state where it can individualise itself while it forms the son of man.

436. Now anyone who closes their disposition to the effect of this spirit — who closes the entrance to their inner being to the language powers of God, in them no inner life can form, not in the here and now and not on the other side at all, and hence this sin is never forgiven, can never be forgiven, as little as someone who rejects any nourishment is to be saved from death by starvation.

437. This apodictic necessity is made perhaps yet more graphic by a parable.

438. A boy can sin against his teacher in school if he is disobedient to the teacher and mocks him. This wrong is the sin against the father and can be atoned for to the extent that the student just recognises his poor behaviour and asks for forgiveness.

439. But he can also sin against the son if he namely misuses what he has learnt in school and uses it for evil ends. Remorse and reversal is still possible here.

440. But if he sins against the spirit of the teacher, i.e. if he does not take up the spirit of the teacher into himself, i.e. if he

Part 3: The Evidence of Sacred Scripture

learns nothing in school, then there is no forgiveness anymore, neither during the schooldays, nor after their end. During the schooldays he finds no forgiveness because he must be constantly rebuked and punished. After discharge from school, however, no remorse can replace for him what he did not learn in his youth.

441. Thus it is with the inner life. To the extent humans do not take up the spirit of God in themselves, to that extent they obtain no inner life. But if they do not obtain the inner life, then they cannot be happy in the here and now, and on the other side they reliably go towards the dissolution, the destruction, the nothing from which we have all arisen.

442. Who is it that has made the human race believe that immortality comes of its own accord, irrespective of whether they have here taken up immortal powers into themselves, or not. Through what law of nature, through what Biblical text is such a contradiction justified?! How long, you people, do you want to still be led around on the fool's errand of self-invented hypotheses!!! — — —

443. Does it not then stand written, however, that the good go to heaven, the evil to hell, John 5:29, you will respond to me.
To which I reply: Do you also know what good is? Do you also know what evil is? — Do you know where heaven is and where hell is? And what, I ask, then happens with those who are neither good nor evil? What happens then with those indifferent everyday people who are too idle for good and too cowardly for evil — what happens then with those pigs whose highest delight is the muck of the earth?!

444. Does it not stand written:
"I will spue thee out of my mouth"? Revelations 3:16.
And furthermore: I will burn the chaff*, cut down the barren tree†, throw away the bad fish‡, and "Because strait is the gate, and narrow is the way, which leadeth unto life, and few there be that find it."§
"If a man abide not in me, he is cast forth as a branch, and is withered". John 15:6.

---

* [Tr.: cf. Matthew 13:40.]
† [Tr.: cf. Matthew 3:10.]
‡ [Tr.: cf. Matthew 13:48.]
§ [Tr.: Matthew 7:14.]

"But he answered and said, Every plant, which my heavenly Father hath not planted, shall be rooted up." Matthew 15:13.
"but whosoever hath not (the inner life), from him shall be taken away even that he hath (the outer life)." Matthew 13:12.
I will kill the unfaithful winegrower, Matthew 21:41, and kill the opponents and murderers of my servants, Matthew 22:7.
"But they which shall be accounted *worthy* to obtain that world, and the resurrection from the dead", etc. Luke 20:35. Must there consequently not also be unworthy who forfeit immortality?
It stands written finally:

Whatsoever a man soweth, that shall he also reap.*
Now if a human has sown for his entire life trumpery, vanity, nullity, transience, can he then harvest abidingness, *immortality*?
The good produce a heavenly rebirth in themselves and live on as brothers of Christ in the kingdom of the Father.
The evil produce a hellish rebirth in themselves, and of them it stands written: their worm dieth not, and the fire is not quenched. Mark 9:44. It cannot, however, lie outside the realm of the possible that the worm transforms itself into a pupa and this transforms into a butterfly, and that the fire, even if late, changes into the light of true knowledge and reconciliation with God, even because Christ expressly said that the sins against God, the Father, and against the son can obtain forgiveness.
Against that, nowhere is there talk of an unconditional immortality and there cannot be either, because those who have sinned against the spirit of life, i.e. anyone who does not believe in, seek, wish for, and awaken any inner life, who also does not desire any, is burnt like chaff, must wither like a vine, their house is built on sand, and if then the wind of death blows, then it will collapse and its place will not be found anymore.
Those who believe that destruction is not punishment enough for the indifferent everyday human should consider that there is none greater and more justified. The tepid man who buried the pound entrusted to him in the earth, i.e. in the earthly,

---
*   [Tr.: Galatians 6:7.]

Part 3: The Evidence of Sacred Scripture

and obtained no interest for eternity from it, to him in just as just a manner the pound is taken away again and he is delivered to dissolution.* That to repay this sin of omission out of vengeance with torture and pain would be unjust, that is only a passionate human idea and is not to be united with the idea of eternal justice — and hence stands also in direct contradiction to the clear sentences of sacred scripture.

445. Oh, that I might only with this text bring a thousand husbands and fathers to sacrifice a few hours just daily to the letter practice, how soon would the physiognomy of the land change!

446. Firstly the worries over sustenance would stop. Nothing draw humans so close to the earth as when they, more unfree than an animal, must fear for their earthly nourishment. Anyone who by the letter practice opens their disposition to the language powers of God obtains the blessing of God, and where this occurs lack can arise as little as someone can freeze who sits behind a warm stove.

447. As it then stands written: I have been young, and now am old; yet have I not seen the righteous forsaken, nor his seed begging bread. Psalm 37:25. Matthew 6:33.

448. Then the illnesses would stop, for the power of the word is not in vain called the *holy* spirit which makes whole from all afflictions, and this healing power penetrates the entire body and first makes it physically sound, for only in a sound body can the inner life develop beneficially. And the healing power of the word would protect and preserve those thousands, and even if entire cities were to die out in a plague.

449. For all that which the earthly body needs, those who seek the inner life through the letter practice do not need to worry, because Christ said: But seek ye first the kingdom of God, and his righteousness; and *all the other things* shall be added unto you. (Matthew 6:33.)

450. With persistently continued practice, the new tongues would finally arise in humans, it would begin to speak in them. As soon as they were to find themselves alone, they would hear loud thoughts in themselves, would be surprised over the liveliness of the words and feel driven to express

---

*   [Tr.: Matthew 25:14–30.]

these thoughts. The expressed thoughts, however, would first penetrate into their disposition after a little time and make the stirring and billowing of the word still clearer.

451. Now the truths of the Christian religion would begin to dawn at once in them. There where they previous saw puzzles and miracles, now the gentlest simplicity will confront them. And this gentleness and this simplicity will make them cheer with joy.

452. And now there would be no stopping anymore. They would share the joy of their hearts with their families and speak in and with their family about the miracle of the inner life.

453. But in the moment when you *speak* about it, a new life begins in the family whose members would form a circle whose centre would be the love for God. And this love would spur them on with superhuman power to seek the spirit of God incessantly. The letter practice would by itself become so familiar to each of them, far better than you are capable of teaching it. They would learn to work the letters during all professional activity and thereby approach the sanctum of God ever more and more.

454. But if it were now to happen thus in thousands of families, then this activity could not remain hidden. You would first speak of it in society with intimations, and as soon as you also found yourself with others of the same mind, the happy condition would finally come close when you would not speak anymore exclusively of politics, of the weather, of earthly business activity — no, it would also be permitted in every educated society, even in the salons, to speak of — God and eternity — — of the inner life.

455. In the moment, however, when that happens, the entire atmosphere would roar and tremble from jubilation and bliss, all the spiritual powers would rejoice and cry hosanna in this atmosphere.

456. In the moment when you would be permitted to speak of the inner life and the language powers of God publicly without hate and persecution, without mockery and derision, you would first see what it means:

Part 3: The Evidence of Sacred Scripture

> "But I say unto you, That every idle word that men shall speak, they shall give account thereof in the day of judgment." Matthew 12:36.

457. For even the thoughts which humans express are creative powers (§ 249) which penetrate into their disposition and that of others and make the expressed idea more and more active in the inner being. Hence the envious become more envious, the man of the world ever more vapid, the ambitious in business ever greedier for money.

458. But it is just the same with the inner life. When humans speak of it, the three-fold sacred word of God becomes ever more animated in them until they finally sink down thanking and exulting before the throne of God, their eternal Father.

459. But if you are ever publicly permitted at every bar, in every dancehall, in every concert, in the theatre, on every promenade to speak about the word and the inner life as well as one does in the church, then there would be no silence anymore. Through this public speech the interest in the inner life, in God and eternity would be awakened in all dispositions and the gifts of the holy spirit would be poured out over all flesh.

460. Now finally the old promise:

> "It is written in the prophets, And they shall be all taught of God. Every man therefore that hath heard, and hath *learned* of the Father, cometh unto me." John 6:45.

would come fully true. For anyone who hears the word of God and learns to feel and experience the language powers of God comes to Christ, to the inner life, they arrive at possession of all the spiritual powers, they obtain the gifts of the holy spirit.

461. Now an entirely new life, the life in heaven, would begin.

462. At first envy would vanish. Why even furthermore should the labourer envy the master — the poor the rich? Why? Because he has a better coat on? Because he can tend to his earthly body more? — Oh, that has no worth anymore.

463. You will no longer regard earthly goods anymore as a goal, only as a means. Earthly goods will not stand any comparison at all with the powers of the inner life, and since these powers are accessible to anyone, nobody can envy anyone else.

464. Just as little will anyone think of betraying or stealing from their neighbour, of outwitting them or inflicting bodily harm. There will be no adulterers and no voluptuaries anymore because the beauty of the word enchants and captivates everyone and makes all vital energies subservient to itself.

465. Thus now, that the realm of evil and selfishness should become quite faint and frail, the inner life would first have to strike proper roots. Now the spiritual senses in humanity would awaken. Think of an entire city of utter clairvoyants!!!

466. Then you would know for the first time what it means to pray to God in the spirit and in the truth. Oh we blind leaders of the blind, we think now, when we speak *in thought to* God, that we are speaking in *the spirit with* God. Oh will it then never become day at all, and the morning star rise in our hearts?

467. Without clairvoyance, without inner life, humans do not know at all what it means *to be in the spirit*.

468. But so that these divine powers are awakened in humanity again, are able to strike roots and develop, you must generally dedicate yourself to the activity of the letter practice. The individual cannot obtain the high perfection of the inner life alone. For as long as the individual lives in an atmosphere which becomes pregnant again and again with swear words, with curses and imprecations, with the cries of sorrow of all the oppressed, suffering people, with envy, hate, fury, haughtiness, vanity, trumpery, and futile gossip, and he must therefore breathe in all these hellish language powers — for so long is he like someone who lives in a city where the plague rages — though it may not even kill him — he will not emerge unscathed from it, the snake will certainly bite him on the heel.*

469. Well, you Christian, decide for yourself, set yourself to work, and the word cannot remain a secret anymore.

470. And if finally the baptism of fire thus comes over those who seek the word, and then what Christ said realises itself: "And these signs shall follow them that believe; In my name shall they cast out devils; they shall speak *with new tongues*; They shall take up serpents; and if they drink any deadly

---

* [Tr.: cf. Genesis 49:17.]

thing, it shall not hurt them; they shall lay hands on the sick, and they shall recover." Mark 16:17–18.

471. Then the inner life could not remain isolated anymore. It would become like a wildfire at first over all of Germany and then spread at ever greater speed over the entire earth.

472. Then all heathens will convert to Christ, to the word of life, and pray to and venerate him as their saviour and redeemer.

473. Then God's stick of discipline will stop. There will be no conflagrations and inundations, no abnormal growth, no bad harvests, and no infectious diseases anymore. You will not wage war against each other anymore, all nations will acknowledge and love each other as members of the one family. Then humans will in old age also not become weak, dull, decrepit, and fragile anymore, but instead it will be as with Moses: "And Moses was an hundred and twenty years old when he died: his eye was not dim, nor his natural force abated." Deuteronomy 34:7.

474. Then the enemy — death — would finally be vanquished. Then the gravediggers will stand idle and the cemeteries will be shown to the latest members of the race as historical antiques and curiosities. Then nobody will easily die anymore.

475. That the human now dies — that he, the human, an image of God, becomes prey to the worms, that the human putrefies, an image of horror, of destruction — that the human sinks utterly from his divine descent — into the arms of extreme weakness, of death — that is the greatest triumph of hell — it is the greatest ignominy for human nature, the deepest humiliation. And so deep, so bottomlessly deep has humanity fallen that it considers this ignominy and shame to be — — — natural.

476. Ha, what sort of squalid divinity would it have to be whose image **by the laws of nature** must rot, contaminating the air with death and filling it with miasmas.

477. Away with such disgraceful teaching. Away with such false doctrines which lead us ever deeper into the abyss.

478. Death is only the wages of sin. Now there are, however, actually no other sins at all than those against the spirit. The other sins are actually only misbehaviours, bad childish

pranks, which must certainly be atoned for and again made good, but which do not draw death after them.

479. Had the human never sinned against the spirit, i.e. had he always taken up the language powers of God, the holy spirit, into himself, acknowledged the fruit of the tree of life as nourishment for his inner immortal life and taken it into himself, then he would never have been able to die.

480. The inner life, the son of man, comes from heaven and returns to heaven. Just as Christ as representative of the inner life went with his entire earthly body to heaven, so finally would all humans go to heaven.

481. The earthly body would shrivel up in those regions where the air becomes too thin, dissolve into atoms, and fall back to earth.

482. This sort of transformation would, however, occur without pain, without loss of consciousness, and would be a transformation worthy of the image of God, whereas putrefaction contains everything which can be deplorable, disgraceful, and contemptible.

483. That this time will yet come, the apostle Paul indicates when he said:

> "Behold, I shew you a mystery; We shall not all sleep, but we shall all be changed, In a moment, in the twinkling of an eye, at the last trump". 1 Corinthians 15:51—52.

484. Thus not all humans will die, but they will surely be transformed like the caterpillar transforms into the butterfly; and the same at the time of the last judgement. This judgement signifies here and in the Revelations of John so much as episodes, periods. When the fruit is brought in, then the harvest is here, as soon as the human possesses the son of man in his maturity, the last judgement then sounds for him. Then he can rise into the air, a free son of the primal power, a citizen of the immeasurable universe.

485. If the ascension will one day take the place of putrefaction, then the going to the Father becomes not a day of sorrow and wailing for those left behind, but instead a family celebration.

486. The person born again in Christ will gather their own about them, take leave of them to see them again soon, give them their blessing, admonish them to seek incessantly the

Part 3: The Evidence of Sacred Scripture

spirit of life and to follow them soon. Then he would rise into the air and amidst waving vanish finally from sight.

487. Faith not only in the possibility, but also in the necessity of the inner life would thereby naturally become so familiar that you would not be able to comprehend at all anymore how there could once have been a time when humans had no idea at all anymore of this happy state. But that the ascension must also be possible for all humanity follows from the words of Christ:

488. He that believeth on me (the word, the inner life), *the works that I do shall he do also*; and *greater* works than these shall he do; because I go unto my Father. (John 14:12.)

489. And it moreover stands written: If a man keep my saying, he shall never see death. (John 8:51.)

490. In the most ancient times there were ascensions here and there. The mythologies of all peoples make mention of them. With the Jews, it was achieved apart from Christ by Enoch, Moses, and Elijah. With each of these three the ascension indicated something different — but not to be denied by the impartial.

491. Christ would not have been able to die according to the way of nature, since dying, as already mentioned, is the greatest ignominy, the deepest humiliation of the spiritual nature of humanity.

492. Now since Christ gave himself of his own free will to death by crucifixion, he thus took upon himself our ignominy of his own free will. In our childish stupidity we harbour now the delusion that Christ would have by taking on this ignominy have taken over *all* our sins. That amounts to about as much as if someone who fell into water wanted to believe he could not drown because once a swimming instructor had offered to teach him to swim. Matthew 12:31.

493. To anyone who wants to adhere to such madness, I entrust to the mercy of God who in his wisdom may know the means and ways of setting limits to any aberration.

494. In concluding, a few more words over the communion. Communion cannot directly produce the inner life. To the contrary, it is a magical bond which puts us in rapport with the spirit of Christ and can thereby activate the **belief** in the inner life, in the language powers of God. This belief is neces-

sary in so far as that without belief nobody will make the effort to awaken the inner life in themselves through the letter practice. But to the extent somebody thinks they can free themselves of the letter practice, that the communion must replace everything, I hold out to them the mirror of the history of the world.

495. Communion has up to now preserved Christianity from reversion to a primitive state, from the last bounds of barbarism, and it will also continue to do so; for in conjunction with the communion, the enormous ideal of Christ must be announced, and the influence of this ideal is so all-powerful that the gates of hell do not overwhelm it.

496. But between the current situation and the extreme perfection there is yet a further space which can only be put aside by humans taking up the language powers of God into themselves and also letting the son of man reproduce in themselves.

497. How in the great mind the spiritual works on the physical, or vice versa, is an undisclosed secret to humanity. Thus it is proof that human and spirit cannot be identical, otherwise these processes would have to be clear and understandable to every human (see § 49).

498. Science acknowledges that every stimulus reproduces the senses as far as the brain, that every change in the great mind calls forth a corresponding change in the sphere of our consciousness; — and that the ability to distinguish a *thought* object from a *real* object is only based on the idea that with the first only the brain mass is active — with the second also the sense nerves are active. Science acknowledges furthermore that the stimulus can penetrate not only from the senses into the brain, but also vice versa from the brain into the senses, and that, to the extent this happens, the possibility drops away of being able to distinguish *thought* objects from *real* objects. From that now dreams, fantasy images, and all sorts of tricks of the senses are explained. —

499. To this extent the matter was entirely in order. The men of science, however, take it a step further, arraying (not paying attention that the extremes touch) the history of the prophets and the reborn, and the tricks of the senses of somnambulist, hysterical, and insane people into one and the same

category and declaring both phenomena to be *pathological*. (Matthew 5:22.)

500. The stimulus of the brain in the senses can admittedly, like e.g. with any fever, thank its emergence to physical causes. In this case the product becomes lawless, confusing, and the human usually forfeits their own consciousness. There is no question that this phenomenon must be called *pathological*.

501. The stimulus of the great mind in the senses, however, can also owe its emergence to the **inner life**, and in this case the human will be in full clear consciousness, and **to the degree** his **inner life** is developed, capable of providing information about spiritual and divine truths, about hidden and future things, and indeed because the spirit is a part of God (see § 31 ff.) — with which the human identifies in the inner life through the rebirth, — and indeed because the ability lies in the spirit to know and to recognise everything (§ 43 ff.) and to suck from God nourishment and power incessantly and without stopping.

502. Now although even the reborn, like *Swedenborg*, commit the mistake of considering the activity of their *inner life* to be objects, this mistake is forgivable, and science cannot justify declaring such men to be insane. I make a far greater reproach to such men, like *Swedenborg*, that they have not written down and delivered to us a complete teaching method for ***how** you can obtain the powers of the **inner life** and speak with **God***. *Swedenborg* would have been up to this task, whereas the present writer is only like a child who wants to attempt an enormous task.

503. Humans must learn to speak with God, but not with the universal divinity, with which they do not stand in any direct connection, — but rather with that part of God which comprises their own spirit.

504. To speak with your spirit means, however, feeling the movements of the spirit (see §§ 215–235). This feeling cannot happen any other way than by *seemingly* sensory objects, by figures and words, etc., which those who have made themselves adroit at perceiving the voice of the spirit think to see and hear.

505. These procedures are purely internal (subjective), for which reason even Christ could not stress often enough and strongly enough that the kingdom of heaven is **within** the human.

506. Science by contrast denies the presence of a prophetic talent in humanity and thereby robs humanity of its highest jewel, its worth, its solemnity, its dignity. — For if it is *impossible* that God and human — human and God can speak with one another — then the human is nothing more than a bright animal, and the striving for truth, wisdom, and love for God is a foolish undertaking.

507. The men of science claim: "As much as individual scholars and academics have also put in the effort, not a single case has yet been established in which the feigned powers of sight of somnambulists and hysterical women has not been reduced to deception and fraud."

508. Is it not sad, I ask in response, that bright, thinking, serious, and honest men are not ashamed to want to establish with hysterical females a fact regarding the prophetic power in humans!!!

509. Do you not recall spontaneously the text in the Bible: **"Behold, the days come, saith the Lord God, that I will send a famine in the land, not a famine of bread, nor a thirst for water, but of hearing the words of the Lord: And they shall wander from sea to sea, and from the north even to the east, they shall run to and fro to seek the word of the Lord, and shall not find it."** Amos 8:11–12.

510. We live at present in the time of fulfillment of this tragic prophesy. Nobody knows anymore *how* and *where* you shall seek the *word* of the Lord.

511. One person thinks the Bible is the word of God. — The Bible is only the *written*, not the *living* word of God. The Bible is only the signpost to the living word; but there is nobody who understands this signpost: for the inner life, the living *word* of God has entirely died out.

512. Anyone who believes then that the word of God is exhausted with the Bible claims as much as if you wanted to say that only such houses may be built to which *Euclid* drafted the plans — only such battles fought to which *Julius Caesar*

gave the plan — only such paintings finished as *Raphael* drew, only such symphonies be composed as those by *Beethoven*, etc. The living *word* of God never repeats itself — it is endless in every direction and cannot be replaced by a written book, or exhausted at all.

513. A different party suggests that in the *conscience* the ability to speak with God is exhausted. If that were so, the divinity would in fact be comparable to King Phillip II who was only seen by his children when it was about pronouncing their punishment. For the conscience is found in fact only ever in the society of *sins*. — Does perhaps the conscience also know how to give information about divine secrets, make regulations about important affairs of state, and make announcements over future things?

514. Elijah mocked the priests of Baal because they could obtain nothing from their Baal despite days of screaming. "either he is talking, or he is pursuing, or he is in a journey, or peradventure he sleepeth, and must be awaked", mocked Elijah, 1 Kings 18:27, but it was no help at all. — Our current divine service is similar, a spiritless and lifeless one. Let us make the attempt and beg for mediation in the most sacred and most important affairs of God, Jeremiah 2:28, it will be shown that everything is dead and ossified. — Nevertheless we do not desist from our blindness, fancying to fulfill by an outer ceremony all justice. (Wisdom of Solomon* 15:3.)

515. Woe if science uses the imposture of weak-nerved women as the basis for explaining the nullity of the prophetic power in humans. — Why do such men not seek *in themselves* the voice of the spirit? Do not their own hearts already tell them that the **possibility** must be present that God must be able to speak with humans — and humans with God? And if they feel that such a possibility is not unthinkable (Jeremiah 29:13), why do they not seek it *in themselves* — rather than with hysterical girls where the morbidity is already established in advance — and to whom the gates to imposture are opened?! — And if they then really discover

---

* [Tr.: the Wisdom of Solomon is one of the books of the Apocrypha and not included in the King James Version.]

only imposture (Jeremiah 23:31–29:9), why do they want to as a result deny and dispute humanity's right to

the knowledge of God,

the highest good?!

516. Seek in yourself, there the source of wisdom is (Wisdom of Solomon 7:21–27). In you is the voice of the holy spirit, the living word of God which is to be obtained by eager activity, *by the letter thinking*.

517. Indeed do not believe as if "*to think letters in the feet*" were a mechanical, spiritless work. To the contrary, there is no more purely spiritual activity. For humans thereby set by virtue of their free will the great mind into action, and this activity must propagate the brain by means of the nerves through the entire body as far as the feet. I know no activity which exercises more easily and at the same time more energetically the entire spiritual power of the human: the wanting, thinking, and feeling. Here the proverb truly applies:

"attempting beats studying"

and when someone has practised the letters in the feet for only an hour daily for thirty years with iron persistence, then they will not need any explanation anymore, but rather perhaps feel driven themselves to express and announce the childishly large secret of the incarnation of Christ (*inner life*).

518. Had I the thunderous voice of a seraph who stands before God, I would call out to the human race: "Learn to think letters in your feet. Learn like children the **A B C** of life. Do not sin against the spirit of God, for these sins are never to be atoned for."

519. That which I call out to others, however, I call out no less to myself, for I too lack the true justice, the inner life.

520. And because I do not yet possess the true inner life, I place my hand to my mouth and apologise before God and remain mindful of the text:

Ask, and it shall be given you;
seek, and ye shall find;
knock, and it shall be opened unto you.[*]

---

* [Tr.: Matthew 7:7.]

Part 3: The Evidence of Sacred Scripture

And for so long as until the fulfillment of this promise approaches, let us wait on the future day of our Lord Jesus Christ. Amen.

***

About the Author

Little is known about Karl Kolb (1824–1895). Aside from being a freemason and director of the cotton mill in Bayreuth, he is known to have been a student and disciple of Johann Baptist Krebs who originated the form of letter mysticism discussed in this work.

For more on the ideas of Johann Baptist Krebs, see his work *Paths to Immortality Based on the Undeniable Powers of Human Nature* (now available from this publisher).

www.ingramcontent.com/pod-product-compliance
Lightning Source LLC
Chambersburg PA
CBHW032303150426
43195CB00008BA/557